A Theatre for Spenserians

Papers of the

International Spenser Colloquium

Fredericton, New Brunswick

October 1969

A Theatre
for
Spenserians

Edited by
Judith M. Kennedy and
James A. Reither

UNIVERSITY OF TORONTO PRESS

© University of Toronto Press 1973
Toronto and Buffalo

Printed in Canada
ISBN 0-8020-1776-2
Microfiche ISBN 0-8020-0123-8
LC 74-185720

UK and Commonwealth except Canada
Manchester University Press
316-324 Oxford Road
Manchester M13 9NR England
ISBN 0-7190-0530-2

Contents

Preface

In October 1969, on the occasion of the four hundredth anniversary of Spenser's first appearance in print in Jan van der Noodt's *A Theatre for Worldlings*, a hundred men and women gathered in Fredericton, New Brunswick, to honour this Prince of Poets. The delegates ranged in age and academic status from undergraduate through all ranks to professor emeritus, and represented forty-five universities: twenty-one Canadian, three British, and twenty-one American. The gathering was throughout distinguished for its 'civil conversation.' The courtesy and generosity which governed the mood of all meetings seemed to be a natural consequence of the happy conviction that it is one of the pleasures of civilized life to discuss poetry so intellectually and imaginatively rewarding as Spenser's.

The colloquium was organized around six papers and a panel discussion which gave stimulus and focus to the continuing discussions. The papers, all original contributions, demonstrate the variety and quality of response that Spenser's poetry today elicits. They are presented in this volume in the order in which they were delivered, although not all in quite the same form: Professors Hieatt, Fowler, Hamilton, and Hunter have to a greater or lesser extent expanded or altered some aspects of their papers (but without changing the central thesis).

The title of this volume has been dictated partly by a wish to commemorate the occasion of the colloquium, and partly by the appropriateness of the contents to meanings of the word 'theatre.' This is indeed a book giving a 'conspectus' or 'view' of its subject, but it can be even more accurately described as 'the scene of action' for readers of Spenser's poetry. Millar MacLure's paper – a study in Spenser's attitudes towards history and the passage of time – provides a very appropriate opening for the collection, because it draws extensively on the volume of *Complaints* in which Spenser for the first time published the revised poems of *A Theatre for Worldlings* under his own name. A. Kent Hieatt and Alastair Fowler are both concerned with large structural patterns in *The Faerie Queene*, but in different ways which tend towards different ends (though not towards contradictory conclusions). William Nelson's essay directs us towards exploring how Spenser's humour controls his narrative illusion. A.C. Hamilton and G.K. Hunter both concentrate their attention on Spenser's rhetoric.

In presenting the papers no attempt has been made to override the preferences of individual contributors in the spelling of quotations. The papers therefore give a spectrum of current attitudes towards the suitable treatment of Spenser's text, from the entirely conservative to the individually modernized.

The panel discussion, chaired by Waldo F. McNeir and entitled 'Research Opportunities in Spenser Studies,' began with Dr McNeir's remarks on 'The Present State of Spenser Studies,' which surveyed Spenser entries in the annual *PMLA* bibliography from 1961 through 1968 and provided thumbnail reviews of thirteen of the more significant book-length studies of Spenser's works published during the same period. The panel members, A. Kent Hieatt, Donald Cheney, K.W. Gransden, and Alastair Fowler, each outlined areas which he felt needed further study. Because this panel discussion – delightfully provocative and informative event that it was – made a vital contribution to the success of the colloquium, we deeply regret that it is not possible to print a transcription of those proceedings in this volume. We can be pleased, however, that a means of continuing the exchange of ideas and information there initiated has now been provided by the *Spenser Newsletter* (edited by Professors Hieatt and Bieman of the University of Western Ontario).

Thanks are due to more people than can be named for making possible the holding of the colloquium. We are grateful to

Mr K.W. Gransden of the University of Warwick, who at short notice came to Fredericton to read the paper of his colleague Professor Hunter, and who made a large personal contribution to the success of the colloquium. We are very happy to acknowledge our most comprehensive debt in thanking the Canada Council, the University of New Brunswick and President Mackay, and St Thomas University and President D.C. Duffie for their indispensable support of the colloquium, which extended far beyond merely providing the money. Both universities made available facilities and tolerated considerable inconvenience in order to accommodate the events of the colloquium during term. Students and faculty from both universities combined in generous assistance. The organizing committee was drawn from both universities, and the editors thank the other members of this committee for their long-continuing and invaluable help: M.J. Taylor (UNB) and W.R. Gair (UNB), and W.C.D. Pacey (UNB) and R.F. Kennedy (STU). This book has been published with the help of grants from the Humanities Research Council of Canada, using funds provided by the Canada Council, the University of New Brunswick, and St Thomas University. We should also like to thank Miss J. Jamieson of University of Toronto Press for all her work in arranging for publication of this volume.

J.M.K.   J.A.R.   *St Thomas University, Fredericton*

A Theatre for Spenserians

Spenser and the ruins of time

MILLAR MacLURE

I dreamed about a man who lived by himself in a landscape of crumbling stones. He spent a great deal of his time, without much success, trying to reconstruct in his mind the monuments and the buildings of which the scattered stones were the only vestiges. He vaguely remembered some kind of oral tradition to the effect that a city had stood there once. And a still vaguer tradition: or perhaps it was a dream inside the dream: that the people who had built the city, or their descendants, were coming back eventually to rebuild it. He wanted to be around when the work was done.

Ross Macdonald, *The Barbarous Coast*[1]

The epigraph for this essay is taken from an American detective story in the tradition of Hammett and Chandler. The dreamer, the hero, is a kind of Artegall working in a world from which Astraea has fled, a Babylon, a House of Pride, once the city of the angels. Spenser the Christian would understand and approve the implications of this vision, but add a postscript: Here we have no continuing city, but seek one to come. Spenser the poet would recognize that the 'dream inside the dream' is a 'palace of art,' a cosmopolis of the imagination, a city of words.

'Time the destroyer is time the preserver': this might well stand as an epigraph for Spenser's *The Ruines of Time*, in which oblivion is defeated by the eternizing power of the poet, and by the 'iust labours' of the antiquary. Perhaps there was some memory of Petrarch's *Triumph of Time* (translated by E.H. Wilkins):

> I saw folk moving onward quietly,
> Free from the fear of Time and of his rage,
> Historians and poets guarding them.[2]

But later, in the same piece, it is said that

> Time dissolves not only visible things,
> But eloquence, and what the mind hath wrought.[3]

A second paradox, in the title itself: the ruins of time are simply the vestiges of the past, in buildings, manners, laws, traditions, which may be interpreted by the historian; or, the ruins of time are sombre evidences of the sway of mutability, to be interpreted by the poet as myth-maker. The resolution of the paradox is possible only through consideration of the providence of God, whose judgments upon human glory may be particular and exemplary, but whose ordinary way of working is to draw all things into his timeless Self, into the artifice of eternity.

I shall deal with Spenser as historian and as poet, and return finally to *The Ruines of Time*. But, first, of Time itself, and Memory.

When a man of Spenser's generation gazed by night upon the starry heavens, observing the orderly procession of the constellations across the vault, his mind was not seriously troubled by notions of infinity. Man had named God's lights, as Adam had named His animals, and they moved, an army of unalterable law, according to certain rules which the Stagirite had been clever enough to find out. It is true there were some serious discrepancies between the observations of antiquity and those of present times, but these could be solved either by an intricate mathematics, or, as in the proem to Book v of *The Faerie Queene*, by recourse to analogical theory: the decay and disorder of human institutions is reflected in, indeed is signalled by, disorder in the heavens. Most of us, and perhaps particularly the extraordinary number of people who seek to guide their lives by the stars' influences, still inhabit this domestic universe. There are two hundred practising astrologers in Manhattan, for we live in a new Middle Age of anarchy and superstition and crusade. The thoughtful layman (and Spenser was one, in his time) is in our time invited, indeed forced, to reflect that when he looks at the stars at night he is looking into an unimaginable past, that the light his little primitive camera receives (his eye, that prime instrument of the soul, of love and wonder) has taken a long journey across the deeps of time, and its source is now not what it was: the science of the astronomer is the art of memory.

Inside the horizon of our immediate, planetary experience, we are aware of a sequence of geological time which, in its depth, its carbon-dating of memory, its intermediate adjustments of the time-scale (e.g., for such monuments as Stonehenge and New Grange), and its relegation of the biblical *cursor mundi* to myth, is almost wholly foreign to the sixteenth-century imagination of nature and man's works. Dr Glyn Daniel has observed that in what he calls 'the pre-archaeological period' it was assumed on the evidence of scripture that everything had to belong to something and to something clearly named and historical. The Pentateuch made antiquity into a kind of human family album. Yet to hold a stone age arrowhead in your hand contracts time which at the same moment is open to a past almost beyond imaginative recovery. The life history of the liver fluke suggests to us a creative intelligence which delights in its own complexity, and the trauma of birth persuades us unconsciously of a special creation.

Post-sixteenth-century Western science conceives of Time in linear terms, in undulating sequence, 'Like as the waves make towards the pebbled shore.' But the traditional metaphors for Time are circular, returning, and intimate: the spool, the loom, the wheel, the sickle. So we dwell in divided and distinguished worlds: the world of apparently arbitrary numbers and the world of elemental words. This division, which frightened Pascal, God's gambler, and has in our time reduced philosophy to a parlour game or a social science, does not seem to have troubled Spenser, who saw, or chose to see, human experience in terms of what C.S. Lewis has called 'the discarded image.' His numbers, his threes, sevens, nines, and their multiplications, are God's numbers, by the aid of which the poet's wordy craft, with its recurrences of rhyme or quantity, imitates the universal harmony created by the Word. What Spenser thought of all this, in the intervals he enjoyed, in a busy public life, for reflection, cannot be our concern. All we know is that he chose, and very early in his life, to translate, by the *imitation* he had learned in school, the genres, the formulas, the patterns of words *which worked* (had worked for the French and Italian learned poets), into a mythology for Tudor Englishmen. Spenser was not a philosopher, but he had what Wordsworth called 'the philosophic mind,' which is not the same thing, but rather what exasperated source-hunters have called eclecticism. Everything is relevant. As Renwick observes in a finely disinterested comment: 'That Spenser follows Aristotle generally in the Book of Justice by no means precludes his following Boethius or Plato, the Hebrew prophets, the institutes of chivalry, or the police system of contemporary Ireland, in any one passage.'[4] But everything is relevant, also, to the apprehension, below thought sometimes, but cultivated generally by schooling in a dying language, of the constant dialectic of change and permanence in the creation. That continuing sense of constancy in inconstancy, in Spenser, has prompted Rosalie Colie to observe that the 'things' and personages in *The Faerie Queene* become, as the great poem works its way into our minds, metamorphosed into their essences. 'They become their being,' as she puts it.[5] Another way (better, less abstract) of putting the same thing is to regard *The Faerie Queene* as an 'art of memory,' a process of *imprinting* on the mind virtues, vices, states of being, as in the tradition described by Frances Yates. And, while we are about it, we should thank Miss Yates for recalling to us that Albertus Magnus held that the melancholy temperament was held to produce good memories, being especially apt to 'receive the impression of images.'[6] I shall turn to Spenser's melancholy later.

When I listen to my graduate students telling me that they want courses in what is 'relevant,' and reflect on the ordinary practice of the affluent society, which is to gobble up the future and defecate the past, it is some solace to remember that the seminal minds of the Renaissance (e.g., Montaigne or Kepler) backed rather uneasily into the future, relinquishing authority for experience only after an intricate calculation of feelings or physical data. Spenser was no virtuoso either: he was the least eccentric of men, and this consideration helps when we are trying to sort out the strains of history in his mind.

There are three of these: Rome, the 'Briton moniments,' and Ireland; and the third is discrete from the others, as we shall see. Spenser was born and brought up in the mediaeval city which lay above and around the Roman Londinium, and he celebrated (but via Camden and Holinshed) the provincial centre at St Alban's. But the ruins of Rome itself, a mediaeval city lately (in 1527) looted and raped by the violent mercenaries of a Catholic prince, were to be found in print and pictures, like the arch of triumph in van der Noodt's *Theatre*, or the verses of Du Bellay. In terms of the procession of empires westward, the Roman succeeded the Assyrian, Persian, and Alexandrian; the ancient boundaries of the Empire were still defended, now against the followers of the Prophet and, as in antiquity, the strangers from the East. While German princes went through a form of marriage with her ghost, Rome was for the humanist the fount of rhetoric and poetry: Cicero and Virgil guarded the iron and the golden gates to the past of the European mind, and opened them to those who through long labours hunted after fame.

Spenser's 'speaking picture' of antique Rome is not the archaeologist's or historian's picture, but rather the image of a Platonic (and Augustinian) *civitas terrena*; there is no meditative survey of the intimacies of a bygone civilization (such as indeed a twentieth-century poet might choose) – remains of villas, apartment blocks, aqueducts, shopping centres (the Sacra Via), baths – but (*RT* 92–6)

> High towers, faire temples, goodly theaters,
> Strong walls, rich porches, princelie pallaces,
> Large streetes, braue houses, sacred sepulchers,
> Sure gates, sweete gardens, statelie galleries,
> Wrought with faire pillours, and fine imageries.

The conflation, in this catalogue, of Roman, mediaeval, and Renaissance elements not only translates Rome into an archetype but establishes it in memory as a House of Pride. (Professor D.C.

7 Spenser and the ruins of time

Allen, in his *Image and Meaning*, has collected, with reference to Prospero's 'cloud-capped towers' and 'gorgeous palaces,' some significant interpretations of the ruins of Rome, before Du Bellay and Spenser, as evidences of spiritual ruin, as a waste place awaiting rebirth, as a primary symbol of mutability.[7]) Du Bellay's catalogue in Spenser's version of his *Antiquitez* gives prominence to

> Triumphant Arckes, spyres neighbours to the skie,
> That you to see doth th'heaven it selfe appall,

an obvious reminiscence of the Tower of Babel; and the Genius of Verulam in *The Ruines of Time*, herself a manifestation of the Virgilian *genius loci* and, by a little topographical manipulation, a Thames maiden, introduces her threnody over Rome in the succession of empires with the 'great seuen headded beast.' Rome was, and is, also 'Rome,' the curse of Protestants, compound of magnificence and superstition, her right arm Spain, her left deviously working on troubled and possibly malicious magnates. Spenser could hardly even have considered a restoration to the days of Mary I; it was inconceivable, intolerable, archaic, over. But the bogey was not only politically useful, but, for a poet (especially for a poet who was a member of the Anglo-Irish Establishment), a curious and indeed powerful figure of the state of his times.

Rome is, then, doubly a 'fallen city': a house of pride built upon the sands of time, opening to the compassionate and imaginative observer the melancholy vistas of mutability, and, as in a sonnet on Venice, which has for us now an added historical dimension, a 'second *Babell* tyrant of the West, / Her ayry Towers vpraised much more high,' like the first fallen 'with the weight of their own surquedry.' 'The antique ruines of the *Romaines* fall' lie strewn in a corner in the dungeons of Lucifera, and the Babylon of popish idolatry falls each time the high heroic enterprise destroys the enemies of the Faerie Queene, on the battlefield or in the soul.

In the mythos of British antiquity, the city of Aeneas is the second Troy, and Troynovant by the Thames the third, and Spenser could see the seeds of Pride in his own realm and perhaps in his own Empress. But the *chronicle of Briton kings, / from Brute to Vthers rayne,* though Spenser from time to time moralizes it by references to treason and discord with a passing reference to 'ambitious Rome,' is mainly inspired by the 'wonder of antiquitie' which Prince Arthur feels. (It is interesting to note that as late as 1674 the Oxford *Almanack* had Brute heading the list of the kings of Britain. Two years later he was replaced by William the Conqueror.) Spenser's Memory is the librarian of the Society of Antiquaries, and has a research assistant; his 'old records from auncient times deriu'd' seem to be rather arbitrarily catalogued (like those of some Cambridge colleges, or those of which Camden so eloquently complained at the beginning of his *Britannia*), but in his way he is an eternizer, as the poet is. For the antiquary, as for the poet, the distinction between myth and history dissolves in the relevance of all that has been experienced or imagined of the human condition.

The book of *'Briton moniments'* lays a legendary pattern over the topography of Britain, from Caerleon to Ludgate Hill; dynasties of throat-clearing names, and evidences of the establishment of a European culture in those islands. The Roman sword crosses the chronicle, and the Incarnation (*FQ* ii.x.50); it invokes the magic of fairy rings and barrows, but it makes Britain a part of Europe too. In the context of the heroic poem, however, what interests the poet most is the return (as in Merlin's prophecy, *FQ* iii.iii) of the decayed kingdom, of 'the antique *Troian* blood.' Merlin's prophecy was not suspect, and indeed there is nothing more Tudor than this mythos of return and restoration. Though the idea of the return, of the seed sprung from burial, the brand inflamed again from the ashes of an overthrow, is indeed universal, and coincides with the doom of Nature in Spenser's *Mutability*, the tough-minded lawyers and landed gentry who created the English Reformation, and, a century later, the dissolution of the royal prerogative, simply plundered Memory's library for precedents, taking a charter here, a phrase there, an ambivalent clause in a proclamation, or a misreading of the Vulgate, to mark the triumph of landed property. So Mr Attorney Cooke, with his Magna Carta; so, eighty years before, the Bishop of Salisbury. But I wonder about Spenser's contexts, and how

9 Spenser and the ruins of time

much he thought about them as contexts. Consider the conversation at Malbecco's dinner table (*FQ* iii.ix).

Paridell, who is entered upon his seduction of Hellenore, in a fabliau-parody of the rape of Helen, utters a sentimental evocation of the 'direfull destinie' of Troy, and of the glories of Paris and Helen, speaking in the clichés of a decayed chivalry. But Britomart wants to hear about Aeneas, and, when the Virgilian tale is told, she rehearses the prophecy of the coming of the 'third kingdome.' Paridell dutifully contributes to the legend of Brute, but his chief aim is to convey an image of glamour to Hellenore. Spenser is concerned to set the contrast between the antique world recalled in indulgent reverie, and the past as pattern of heroic and creative action. The conversation exhibits not only two different aspects of the Troy-matter, but also two characters in a fictional setting; the method is typically Spenserian: he has advanced his story and at the same time re-introduced a major structural and pictorial motif into the whole fabric of his poem.

The symbol of 'history' in the abstract, as it is, for example, an informing element in Eliot's *Four Quartets*, is entirely foreign to Spenser's imagination, but he is almost Spenglerian in the consistency with which he exploits certain *topoi* in his imaging of the past. He is haunted by the spectacle of recurrence and decline, and the whole of *The Faerie Queene* as we have it is really that 'Legend of Constancy' which we have not otherwise; from his classical reading, from the Book of Daniel, from Geoffrey of Monmouth and Holinshed, from Camden 'nourice of antiquitie,' he derived the pattern of civilization as *naming*, making approachable and indeed domestic a Titanic and rude disorder. Running happily through the English rivers in his great masque of the marriage of Thames and Medway in *FQ* iv, he confesses that he cannot tell the 'hidden race' of the Irish rivers.

For Rome never came to Ireland, nor, in Spenser's time, except for a few little enclaves, the ancient customs of the realm of England, so that when Spenser set himself to write a state paper on the problem of 'reducinge that salvage nacion to better gouernment and cyvillitie' in his *View of the Present State of Ireland*, he was, so to speak, free of his conventions. The 'salvage men,' the satyrs of *The Faerie Queene*, and other creatures out of books and emblems, had little place there. Renwick has noted that in Ireland 'he found a conspicuous example of instability'[8] and the relation of the *View* to *FQ* v is conspicuous, but generally Spenser looked at the problem, the land, the people, their traditions and customs in a straight practical way, i.e., the *English* way. Some scholars have found him going at the question according to Jean Bodin's *Methodus*, but, as Renwick says, 'without Bodin his ideas would probably have been much the same.' His programme for Ireland, his defence of Lord Grey, need not concern us here. But he was confronted by a culture or cultures of demonstrable antiquity, and it is worth noting how he took those into his mind.

At the end of the *View* he promises a set of observations on 'the Antiquities of Ireland,' and I must confess I would rather have those than another book of *The Faerie Queene*. Perhaps I look for too much. Renwick, who has been through this matter with exemplary learning and good sense, believed that the MS in PRO (Renwick, pages 258ff.) represents a draft of historical matter drawn from a wider selection of written authorities than Buchanan's *Historia*: the implication is that Spenser's projected work would have been so to speak fleshed out of books, with more information about the Scythians, the Gauls, the 'Africans,' and other presumed founding peoples. But there is enough of sympathetic observation in the *View* to suggest that these notes would have been corrected against observation. Irenius, in the dialogue, is helpful here: he will rely on oral tradition, he says,

> but add my own readinge and out of them both together
> with comparison of tymes, lyknes of manners and customes,
> affinitie of words, & names, properties of Natures and vses,
> resemblances of rightes and ceremonies monumentes of
> Churches and Tombes, and manye other lyke Circumstances
> I doe gather a likelihoode of truth ...

He goes on to mention his authorities, giving most credit to Buchanan, but adding that in the bardic matter and the Irish chronicles there are 'some reliques of the true antiquitie'; Ireland, he adds against an objection, 'hath had the use of lettres verie auncyentlie and longe before England.' And his commendation of the 'sweete wit and good invencion' of the Irish poets shows a nice if condescending liberality of taste.

I know that we have to take into account Yeats's comment, that Spenser 'never pictured the true countenance of Irish scenery, for his mind turned constantly to the court of Elizabeth and to the umbrageous level lands, where his own race was already seeding like a great poppy,' but his *View* is, of course, of the *present* state of that island, and his account of migrations would not be dismissed out of hand by a modern antiquary – or by popular tradition: I have heard Spenser's pattern of the first settlements from the late custodian of the great burial mound at Dowth, and other curious matter besides. The 'wonder of antiquitie' is strong in Spenser. He would have approved John Aubrey's sensitive and prophetic comment, in the next century: '[Ruins] breed in generous minds a kind of pity, and set the thought a-work to make out their magnificence as they were taken in perfection.' Long before him, Samuel Daniel, in his *Musophilus*, had assembled the commonplaces, in his eloquent way, about Stonehenge:

> And whereto serue that wondrous *trophei* now,
>   That on the goodly plaine neare *Wilton* stands?
> That huge domb heap, that cannot tel vs how,
>   Nor what, nor whence it is, nor with whose hands,
>   Nor for whose glory, it was set to shew
> How much our pride mockes that of other lands?
> Whereon when as the gazing passenger
>   Hath greedy lookt with admiration,
>   And faine would know his birth, and what he were,
> How there erected, and how long agone:
>   Enquires and askes his fellow trauailer
> What he hath heard and his opinion:
> And he knowes nothing. Then he turnes againe
>   And looks and sighs, and then admires afresh,
>   And in himselfe with sorrow doth complaine
> The misery of darke forgetfulnesse;
>   Angrie with time that nothing should remain,
> Our greatest wonders-wonder to expresse.

Of course Daniel goes on to speak pretty sharply about the

lies of antiquity – as indeed his namesake (the editor of *Antiquity*) does now. But the wonder is accompanied by its proper corollary, the desire to have the remote past in some order: Spenser is closest to Camden when he is out of England. On ring-forts he is very sound, and he dismisses the folk superstition that the megalithic tombs are 'the ould Geantes tryuettes' (Renwick, pages 101–2); he knows they are the tombs of kings. He dwelt himself among the ruins of later times, at New Abbey and Kilcolman, where the Norman tower still dominates a meadow and a pool. Spenser, typically, referred to his domain as 'Hap Hazard.'

These ruins of time, in Ireland, are as a rule far from monumental; they arise intimately upon a softly repetitious landscape. John Lackland's castle at Trim, which has that rugged magnificence the Normans set up from Ireland to Jerusalem, was no ruin in Spenser's time: he was almost certainly there in early April of 1582;[9] but he probably never saw Steague Fort or Dunbeg. We must remember that he was there before Cromwell, who razed the strongpoints in the name of God. The archaeologists' stratification often does not apply with any consistency in that area, and the 'ragged monuments of times forepast, / All which the sad effects of discord sung' appear, not as in Ate's museum (*FQ* IV.i.21), but diffused in pastures, valleys, and headlands. The conventions of magnificence, the hyperboles of empire have no place there; any place in Ireland is a good place to talk, from Tyrone (who outfoxed Essex that way) to O'Connell, and Spenser, a transplanted English civil servant, recognized this. 'These metinges on hills,' he has Irenius observe just after his bit of scholarship on burial mounds, 'yt is verie inconveniente that any such should be permitted speciallie in a people so evill mynded, as they now bee and dyverselie showe them selues.' Granted the difference of idiom, it would be hard to find a better description from an English point of view of the conversation in an Irish bar, or, for the romantics, within a decayed rath, during the troubles of the 1920s.

Spenser's long meditation on the transience of human institutions, begins, it seems to me, from a centre of constitutional melancholy. This is translated into the great literary and emblematic conventions: *ubi sunt*, the wheel of Fortune (Book VI of

The Faerie Queene is under Fortune, as Book I is under Providence). I know how dangerous it is to attribute to a personal preoccupation the recurring *sententiae* and image patterns of a highly sophisticated craftsman, particularly when his sentiments are echoed by other poets of his time. But it is even more dangerous to take the other way, and turn the poet into a virtuoso of convention. It would be easy to collect from what we know of his personal experience sufficient reminders of the world's vanity to make a Quoheleth of him: indeed he seems to have versified *Ecclesiastes* (whose sombre but airy pronouncements had, I imagine, a great effect on his youthful imagination) as well as the *Canticum canticorum* – a characteristic polarity of passionate interest. Like Eliot, he adopted the pose of the aged eagle (or owl, if you like) very young:

> So now my yeare drawes to his latter terme,
> My spring is spent, my sommer burnt vp quite;

so the pastoral mode of the shepherd in December, and, before, in the November elegy, the sudden lift of the verse, as the poet gathers himself to a congenial theme:

> O trustlesse state of earthly things, and slipper hope
> Of mortal men, that swincke and sweate for nought,
> And shooting wide, doe misse the marked scope:
> Now haue I learnd (a lesson derely bought)
> That nys on earth assuraunce to be sought.

A poet assumes a persona (a term congenial to electronic image-makers and literary critics, especially PH D candidates, but anathema to, for example, Milton, who would have simply replied to it with the strongest expletive his careful self-discipline allowed, and stalked upstairs to bed, feeling the banister) because it fits him: the armour, the soup-and-fish, the lounge-suit, the riding-habit, the farm-labourer's jerkin, the singing robes: the last of these is worn by the poet who is prophetic to a nation, and, if you close your eyes for a moment, the costume will look like a shepherd's cloak, his *skeptron* like a crook. This is Spenser's garb.

He wore it well. He stood, we must remember, at the edge of Europe, in Ireland at the very edge, with nothing beyond him but Tir-an-og, the unchanged country of the young, which he never knew. From this vantage point, a provincial poet looking east down time, he surveyed the inevitable process of change and decay from its sources in the first empires of men to its presence in the uncertain diplomacy of the Elizabethan establishment. He saw it as a law of nature, earthly and celestial, 'Sith onely God surmounts all times decay.' In *The Shepheardes Calender* Colin and his friends pass through the seasons, and in *Colin Clouts Come Home Againe* Colin feels the summer sun and the wintry bite of Eliza's court. Like Shakespeare's Henry v, Spenser idealizes the *timeliness* of the simple life (cf. *FQ* vi.ix.23): to everything there is a season, a time to be born and a time to die, as the wise man said. This is the lesson that old Meliboee teaches Calidore, and one term of the paradox with which Nature puts down Mutability. Time for Spenser, the sixteenth-century poet-moralist, is no absolute, as it is for some of his modern critics, but rather existential, like grace for a Puritan professor (I mean 'professor' in the seventeenth-century sense, of course). Here I return to the double meaning of 'Time' which I noted at the beginning of this essay. For the shepherd, as for the wise man who in his sophisticated Platonic way can look up to 'that soveraine light,' there is a 'safe retyre / Of life' (*FQ* vi.ix.27), since Time is a condition of the human garden, and the dead stalks are the 'ruins of time' from whose seeds they spring again. The vegetable creation is renewed, for Nature's clock is circular. Fortune's clock is marked at 12 and 6, and God's clock has no hands or figures.

I have so far been concerned mainly with such of Spenser's writings as those he might be said to have worked on with complete engagement (though of different kinds), the *View* and *The Faerie Queene*. The poem from which I began, *The Ruines of Time*, is another kind of composition, an assembly of commonplaces rhetorically amplified, and expertly arranged into a kind of unity, not only by the 'numerical composition' which Professor Nelson has noted, but through the juxtaposition of the poet's genres of apprenticeship and the preoccupation with a favourite theme. Some at least of the lost works underwent a metamorphosis, and this is the result.

Twenty years later, in the Sixteenth Song of *Polyolbion*, Drayton was to sing of lofty *Verlam*, 'with Alablaster ... and Porphery adorn'd, / When (welneare) in her pride great *Troynovant* she scorn'd,' and Selden in his notes did not fail to quote Spenser, while locating the source of his error about the course of the Thames, and pointing out what modern excavation has confirmed, the importance and indeed monumental quality of the Roman town.[10] But the ruins, in the literal sense, serve Spenser merely as prelude to his meditation, and his *genius loci* is a very faint Virgilian echo, serving rather as a speaking person, delivering an elegiac oration which is at the same time an anthology of *topoi* on the initial theme: 'Ah what delight ... in earthly thing?' '*Verlame* I was,' she says, and proceeds at once to a theme from *The Wisdom of Solomon* ('... and hereafter we shall be as though we had never been; because the breath in our nostrils is smoke ... Our life will pass away like the traces of a cloud, and be scattered like mist'); from that to the *ubi sunt* motif (ll. 57–77), confirmed by a short history of the past glories of Rome in the 'small Northerne world,' on the banks of Spenser's favourite river, with a tribute to the enduring and eternizing labours of the antiquary Camden.

The genius continues her complaint, but the disguise is next to transparent, as the poet repeats the pattern in terms of the Dudley family, punctuating his melancholy recital, as before, with hortatory aphorisms from his own 'wisdom.' For the loss of 'that gentle River' with its winged ships, the transposition introduces a fine elegy on Sidney, now companion of Orpheus in Elysian fields; for the records of the antiquary, the eternizing power of the poet; and for the pride, 'outragiousnesse,' and 'greedie powre' of past empires, the spite and 'blatter' (a word from the *View*) of evil men, lesser men, specifically Burghley (we think) –

He now is gone, the whiles the Foxe is crept
Into the hole, the which the Badger swept.

The long discourse is changed, by obvious rhetorical transitions, into a little mirror for magistrates, invoking the verdict of history, and applying the lesson in terms appropriate to what is becoming a lay sermon in verse:

Prouide therefore (ye Princes) whilst ye liue,
That of the *Muses* ye may friended bee ...

For the poets stellify their subjects, make myths of them, and myths do not die. The restored city is a palace of art, of 'wise wordes taught in numbers for to runne.' The 'pageants' which follow are 'demonstrations' setting the fallen city, in emblematic terms, against the restored city, figured in microcosm as Sidney in the glass of art. The first set of speaking pictures, of pride, power, and beauty, is derived from biblical images, beginning with the book of Daniel, prophetic of the fall of empires, and reminiscences of the wonders of the ancient world; the sixth and most esoteric pageant seems to refer to the Dudley family. The second set celebrates the entrance into immortality of Sir Philip Sidney. The 'Immortall spirite of *Philisides*' is made 'the heauens ornament,' *translated* (in a double sense) into such appropriate figures as the singing swan, the harp, the winged horse, a coffer hiding precious treasure. The religious analogy is confirmed by the 'curious Coffer,' which holds a treasure 'Exceeding all this baser worldes good,' by the figure of the Bridegroom who comes seeking his Bride, and is combined with the figure of Mercury as psychopomp in the pageant of the removal above the sky of the ashes from the funeral hearse of the dead hero-poet.

Miss Bradbrook has an illuminating comment on the parts of this poem. Emphasizing Spenser's disillusionment in his worldly pursuit of fame, she observes: 'Grief for Leicester was mixed with the bitterness of worldly disillusion; the despair for Sidney could be expressed only in heroic symbols, impersonal visions.'[11] Lament alternates with 'festivity.' In the traditional pattern of the pageants, both public and esoteric, the brazen world of power's fall and fame's ruin is transformed into the golden world of poetic vision.

The phrase 'palace of art,' which frames this discussion, should not be taken in its delusive Tennysonian sense (though all these allusions are instructive) as describing a 'lordly pleasure-house' for self-indulgent contemplation; but it is as exemplary as the ruins of Tennyson's experiment with his aesthetic education. It is, moreover, *historical*, national, like his *Faerie Queene*, designed to 'live with the eternitie of [Elizabeth's] fame.' Having experimented with words, having 'in affecting the Ancients writ no Language,' having created an idiom so distinctive as to lend itself to parody by the infant Pope, he must have understood that even the edifice of words is temporal, and gathered finally into God's silence. Words break down, decay with imprecision, but the river, sustained by the cycle of nature, runs by Cleopolis. And the poet, after his great achievement, must still, in the memory of him, be sustained by the pretentious preface of his first collaborators, my excuse for this paper:

> Hereunto have I added a certain Glosse or scholion ... These my present paynes if to any they be pleasurable or profitable, be you iudge ...

NOTES

1 Ross Macdonald, *The Barbarous Coast* (New York: Alfred A. Knopf, Inc., 1956). Copyright © Kenneth Millar, 1956.
2 *The Triumphs of Petrarch* (Chicago, 1962), p. 98.
3 Ibid., p. 100.
4 W.L. Renwick, *Edmund Spenser: An Essay on Renaissance Poetry* (London, 1925), p. 161.
5 Rosalie Colie, *Paradoxia Epidemica* (Princeton, 1966), p. 350.
6 Frances A. Yates, *The Art of Memory* (London, 1966), p. 69.
7 Don Cameron Allen, *Image and Meaning* (Baltimore, 1960), pp. 62–6.
8 *A View of the Present State of Ireland*, ed. W.L. Renwick (London, 1934), introduction.
9 A.C. Judson, *The Life of Edmund Spenser* (Baltimore, 1945), p. 104.
10 *The Works of Michael Drayton*, ed. J.W. Hebel et al. (Oxford, 1961), IV, 322–4.
11 Muriel C. Bradbrook, 'No Room at the Top: Spenser's Pursuit of Fame,' in *Elizabethan Poetry*, Stratford-upon-Avon Studies 2 (London, 1960), p. 106.

Three fearful symmetries
and the meaning of *Faerie Queene* II

A. KENT HIEATT

Two recent developments in the investigation of numerical patterns in Spenser's poetry may advance our understanding of his work.

In his recent paper on *Amoretti*[1] O.B. Hardison made use of Alexander Dunlop's new theory of a calendrical sequence, and of a bilateral, or reciprocal, numerical symmetry, in this sonnet sequence. The discovery appears to necessitate a revision of our previous notions of the intended total impact of *Amoretti*, to emphasize the continuity between *Amoretti* and *Epithalamion*, and to confirm my own contentions about the numerically symbolized day and year of *Epithalamion* (although not, certainly, my entire interpretation of this phenomenon).[2] Dunlop announced his discovery in a preliminary note[3] and published a much fuller study in a collection of essays edited by Alastair Fowler.[4] I have drawn further conclusions from Dunlop's discovery in my tally of a decade of investigations of Spenser's numbers and also in a new article.[5]

In the second place an article by Baybak, Delany, and Hieatt[6] offers solid evidence for a certain kind of numerical structure in *The Faerie Queene*. It thus seems to confirm the contention of Fowler, in *Spenser and the Numbers of Time*,[7] that numerical composition exists in *The Faerie Queene*. The total configuration of Fowler's theory is by no means demonstrated by the Baybak, Delany, and Hieatt article, although examples of one of the devices which he discussed – namely, the centre-points of individual books of *The Faerie Queene* – reappear, in somewhat different locations and attire from the ones assigned by him. Their essay appears in modified form in Fowler's collection.[8] This paper describes what some of the consequences of their discovery seem to be for our understanding of the first three books of *The Faerie Queene*. In this connection I am mainly concerned to give a new interpretation of Book II.

The discovery itself can be briefly and simply described. In each of the three books of *The Faerie Queene*, in the edition of 1590, the mathematically central stanza or stanzas contain a reference which may be thought of as central to the book, and which relates to the phrase 'in the middest,' or 'in the midst.' Because there has been some outcry against Fowler's alternative systems of stanza-counting I should say at the outset that, in each of the three books, the regular stanzas of all twelve cantos are counted as they appeared in 1590. The stanzas of the proems and the argument-stanzas are not counted. I shall now give you the evidence for each book in the order which finally brought absolute conviction to Baybak, Delany, and Hieatt.

The Garden of Adonis in III.vi has as its geographically central feature the hill or mount within which Venus preserves in concealment for her own joy Adonis, the generative principle of the Garden, and beneath which the boar of death is imprisoned. We are now probably all agreed that, not only in the Garden, but also in terms of female anatomy, this Mount is central, for it is plainly the *mons Veneris*. The stanza in which the discussion of it begins (43) opens with the phrase that I have already indicated:[9]

> Right in the middest of that Paradise,
>   There stood a stately Mount, on whose round top
>   A gloomy grove of mirtle trees did rise,
>   Whose shadie boughes sharpe steele did never lop,
>   Nor wicked beasts their tender buds did crop ...

This stanza is the middle one of Book III, preceded by 339 stanzas and followed by 339 stanzas, in the edition of 1590. The evidence that Spenser intended to erect a centre-point here, in the arithmetical sense, is thus very strong.

In Book II the mathematical centre is to be found in canto vii, the episodes connected with the Cave of Mammon. After passing through the cave itself, and the chamber of Philotime, Guyon is led to the Garden of Proserpina, the scene of his final temptations before leaving the lower regions. A self-contained unit of three stanzas (53, 54, 55) describes the central features of this garden: that is, the silver seat, which Mammon later tempts Guyon to occupy, and the tree with golden apples (also used to tempt Guyon) which overshadows it. The mathematical centre of Book II is in the midst of these three stanzas, but in order to include the significant phrase, it is necessary to begin with the first of them, thus:

> The *Gardin of Proserpina* this hight;
> And in the midst thereof a silver seat,
> With a thicke Arber goodly over dight,
> In which she often usd from open heat
> Her selfe to shroud, and pleasures to entreat.
> Next thereunto did grow a goodly tree,
> With braunches broad dispred and body great,
> Clothed with leaves, that none the wood mote see
> And loaden all with fruit as thicke as it might bee.

The following two stanzas, completing this unit, enumerate the most famous of the golden fruit derived from here; then, at the end of the unit of three stanzas, there is a definite change in point of view, beginning, 'The warlike elfe, much wondred at this tree ...' The three stanzas in question are preceded by 340 stanzas, and followed by 340 stanzas, in the 1590 edition.

In Book 1 the mathematical centre is likewise in canto vii. Since there are an even number of stanzas in the book, there are two central stanzas instead of one, preceded by 295 stanzas and followed by 295 stanzas. These two (12 and 13) detail the striking down of Redcross by the giant Orgoglio, after Redcross has been weakened by drinking the waters of Diana's recreant nymph and has paid court to Duessa. The first of these two stanzas reads as follows:

> The Geaunt strooke so maynly mercilesse,
> That could have overthrowne a stony towre,
> And were not heavenly grace, that him did blesse,
> He had beene pouldred all, as thin as flowre:

But he was wary of that deadly stowre,
And lightly lept from underneath the blow:
Yet so exceeding was the villeins powre,
That with the wind it did him overthrow,
And all his sences stound, that still he lay full low.

The second stanza continues with the long simile ('As when ...')
of the cannon that seems to daunt with its breath those who
escape its ball.

Where is the significant phrase? It occurs seven stanzas
before this, in stanza 5, in what has several times been described
as an episode emblematic of Redcross's situation here: the reason
that he has grown faint before he has finished his task (even
though he has made a good beginning, most recently in leaving
the House of Lucifera) is that he has drunk from the spring which
Diana has made debilitating as a punishment to its nymph, who,
while following Diana in the hunt, (i.vii.5)

quite tyr'd with heat of scorching ayre
Sat downe to rest *in middest* of the race:
The goddesse wroth gan fowly her disgrace,
And bad the waters, which from her did flow,
Be such as she her selfe was then in place.
Thenceforth her waters waxed dull and slow,
And all that drunke thereof, did faint and feeble grow.

As the reader sees, the evidence has been ranged in order of
descending cogency, but it is still extremely strong. It is unlikely
to be by chance that the catch-phrase 'in the middest,' or 'in the
midst,' occurs in relation to these three passages, for all variants
of this preposition plus its object occur only eleven times in the
approximately two thousand stanzas of the first edition of *The
Faerie Queene*. It is true that the concepts involved – spatial cen-
trality in II and III, and the point half-way through a task in I –
might have summoned up the words, but there are many other
important parallels in these three passages and their contexts,
written by a poet who, we seem to be agreed, has composed
numerically elsewhere.

Each of the three episodes is located in a variety of *locus amoenus*. In III, in the Garden of Adonis, the surroundings of the Mount are the greensward, the trees with fruit and with blossoms of fresh colour decking 'the wanton Prime,' and the joyful birds. In II there is a kind of *locus amoenus* in reverse in the Garden of Proserpina: the stream (a 'blacke flood') and the vegetation: the garden here is said in stanza 51 to be 'goodly garnished / With hearbs and fruits' (although 'direful deadly blacke both leafe and bloom'); there are the golden apples of the central tree. In I the fountain with its 'bubbling wave' beside which Redcross and Duessa disport themselves is seconded by a 'breathing wind,' 'trembling leaves,' and 'cherefull birds' chanting 'sweet musick.'

In addition, the central space in each of the three episodes corresponds to the archetype of the protected withdrawing place for privacy and pleasure. In III a ring of myrtle trees in stanza 43 'like a girlond compassed the hight,' shading it from heat; and then in stanza 44 'in the thickest covert of that shade / There was a pleasant arbour,' made by a natural knitting together of tree branches, eked out with twining vines so as to form an enclosure impenetrable to sun or wind. It is here that Venus enjoys Adonis in delicious privacy. In II the central, silver seat, ready to tempt Guyon, is in stanza 53 'With a thicke Arber goodly over dight,' from which in turn grows densely the tree which overshadows all the island-garden and surrounds it on all sides with branches that hang down into the river of Cocytus. The notion of the pleasurable effects of shade in the total gloom of the Infernal Regions looks like a familiar Spenserian device (so outrageous to those who are coming to him for the first time) to create a parallel, as does the notion of the pleasure which Proserpina derives from sitting there:

> And in the midst thereof a silver seat,
> With a thicke Arber goodly over dight,
> In which she often usd from open heat
> Her selfe to shroud, and pleasures to entreat.

With one hand, it seems to me, Spenser gives us the notion of guilty pleasures, or sexual ones (with his plural substantive), and consequently a closer parallel to the pleasures of Redcross and

Duessa and of Venus and Adonis; with the other (we must acknowledge with our waking minds, thinking of the upright position of the chair) he goes no further than to give us the pleasures of retired privacy and (since he insists on it) cool shade.

In 1, as soon as Duessa joins Redcross by the fountain, the enclosure, again like a garland, is summoned up, in stanza 4, cutting them off from the eye of heaven and men.

> Unkindnesse past, they gan of solace treat,
>   And bathe in pleasaunce of the joyous shade,
>   Which shielded them against the boyling heat,
>   And with greene boughes decking a gloomy glade,
>   About the fountaine like a girlond made;
>   Whose bubbling wave did ever freshly well,
>   Ne ever would through fervent sommer fade.

Their pleasures continue without care until the arrival of Orgoglio.

There are other striking contextual parallels. One is, in the context of the central passage in the Garden of Proserpina, the mythological exemplary catalogue of deadly plant life and of heroically obtained golden apples and, in the corresponding context of the Garden of Adonis, the mythological exemplary catalogue of flowers into which sad lovers had been transformed. Another is the need for divine grace, and the arrival of Arthur in the role of a saviour, 1 / for Redcross rendered faint by the water and imprisoned by Orgoglio, and 2 / for Guyon as the prey of Pyrochles and Cymochles, after the stress of his Infernal journey has made him fall into a faint at its termination. But principally the verbal, narrative, and other correspondences are such, I think, as to make us believe that Spenser was concerned in the edition of 1590 to compose numerically at least in one sense – to create three architectonically symmetrical structures by placing at their mathematical centre-points three climactic and in many ways parallel stanzas.

It seems to me likely that Spenser's essential formal aim in the matter of these midpoints was that the significant situation itself should be precisely at the centre, not that the description of the setting and the catch-phrase should be there, although they would have to be nearby, since the situations which are central occur in the midst of these landscapes themselves.

But what of the edition of 1596? By our method of counting stanzas Books iv, v, and vi do not reveal centre-points which are obviously significant. Furthermore, the changes in the first three books in that edition partly remove the significance of their centre-points. Book ii remains as before, but the addition in Book i of a new stanza 3 in canto xi moves the exact centre-point not to the stanza of Orgoglio's overthrow of Redcross, but to the single stanza (i.vii.13) following it, in which we read the simile of the cannon; and the new conclusion of Book iii moves the centre-point back one stanza, to iii.vi.42, beginning, 'There is continuall spring, and harvest there / Continuall ...' Perhaps some accommodation, like the one according to which not one but the three stanzas in ii.vii are already thought of as the central unit, might have occurred to Spenser, but I see no way of demonstrating this. The disparity, coupled with the fact that, as Fowler's figures show, there are a round 18,000 lines[10] (by one kind of counting) in the three books of 1590, but what sound to me like an adventitious 15,741 lines in Books iv, v, and vi, encourages me to conjecture that Spenser, sometime after preparing the edition of 1590, either lost interest in his numerical structures, or sophisticated them to another level. I repeat, this is a guess. There is a curious parallel. The centre-point which Gunnar Qvarnström finds[11] in *Paradise Lost* works only for the earlier, ten-book version, not for the later twelve-book one.

Now, what appears to be a successful demonstration of numerical structure in a part of *The Faerie Queene*, partially seconding Fowler, is interesting, but how much weight can be put upon the newly discovered structures as aids to the interpretation of this poem?

If the likelihood that Spenser intended this numerical parallelism is conceded, our position is still not radically different from what it was before. We have a new datum suggesting other kinds of parallelism between these three episodes more strongly than the known data would have permitted before, but this discovery is only one piece of evidence. We must attend as firmly as ever to the rhetorical and narrative and figurative pressures in Spenser's text, because we have no warrant otherwise for judging either the *direction* or the *extent* of the posited parallelism.

Probably our chief task ought to concern the Garden of Proserpina and the Cave of Mammon in Book II. I believe that, concerning many of the main lines of the Redcross-Duessa-Orgoglio episode in Book I and of the Garden of Adonis in Book III, there is a large measure of agreement today, even though this agreement used not to exist. Where relevant, this agreement confirms the importance of the discovered centre-points. Nothing that I say here is going to change that agreement very much. In the case of Book I most of us are probably agreed that Redcross has surmounted one kind of *superbia*, root of all other sins, in the House of Lucifera, only to fall prey to pride in another form in the case of Orgoglio; that his thus falling to Orgoglio is the culminating effect of his parting from Una or Truth; that his association with Duessa is with untruth and with either the false flesh that weakens him for the assault of sin, or with one form of the pride of the flesh itself, of which a parallel symbol is Orgoglio; that the indication of the presence of grace (at i.vii.12.3) even in his defeat is to be associated with Arthur's rescue of him; that his subsequent reunion with Una begins his interrupted climb towards wholeness, after he reaches a low point in the book in the submission to Orgoglio. Similarly, in the matter of the Garden of Adonis in Book III, there seems to be fairly general agreement on the following points: that the importance of physical love as the guarantor of the earthly world's survival against death, through our eternity in mutability, is here announced and is central to this book of chaste love; that the accordance with Nature, and the harmonious, unjealous character of this love, is contrasted to a corresponding quality in other allegorical scenes (chiefly the Bower of Bliss) and complemented by still other such scenes (chiefly the Isle of Venus) elsewhere in *The Faerie Queene*; that Amoret, brought up in the company of Pleasure, is indeed the pattern of chaste female affection in its open and partly passive aspect in Book III, despite her troubles on behalf of Scudamor.

There is not, however, any such agreement about the Cave

of Mammon in general and the Garden of Proserpina in particular in Book II. There is more here to investigate, and we may now be in a better position to investigate it. One likely surmise which is new to the discussion, and that we can now contribute, is that the Garden of Proserpina itself is, or at some point in Spenser's gestation of it was designed to be, as crucial as the corresponding passages in I and III, and that there is quite possibly some parallel with one or both of them.

The heart of what I want to put before you in the rest of this paper is a new reading of what Spenser was trying to embody in Book II, given the new datum that the Garden of Proserpina episode is as pivotal as the Garden of Adonis or the overcoming of Redcross by Orgoglio. This reading possesses at least the virtue of simplicity. There are really two points.

The first is that Spenser continues throughout Book II the twofold division of intemperance which he makes at the beginning in Guyon's comment on Mordant and Amavia in the episode concerning Ruddymane: (II.i.57.7–9)

> The strong it weakens with infirmitie,
> And with bold furie armes the weakest hart;
> The strong through pleasure soonest falles, the weake
> through smart.

The later representatives of a kind of disdainful and irascible contentiousness and ambition are the full development of bold fury, weakness, and smart here; the strong who are weakened with infirmity through pleasure are those who, later in the book, turn aside into sensual indulgence. Essentially this underlying duality, with the addition of much new moral and psychological material, characterizes the pairs Elissa (disdainfully unapproachable and contentious) and Perissa (sensually loose); Acrates' sons Pyrochles (fierily contentious) and Cymochles (fluidly falling into sensual indulgence); and Impatience and Impotence, the two supporters of Maleger in his struggle with Arthur to take over the House of Alma.

The second point of my interpretation has to do with Guyon's successful conquest of what I believe to be two chief embodiments of these two classes of irrational and passionate intemperance. Arthur evidently overcomes the two forms at the same time, in the struggle with Maleger and his two helpers and, in another sense, in defeating Pyrochles and Cymochles, sons of Acrates, simultaneously. Guyon, however, overcomes them one at a time: he defeats sensual intemperance embodied in Acrasia and her Bower of Bliss, with its wide open gate, at the end of Book II; he defeats disdainful ambitiousness embodied in Mammon (first and above all disdainful) and his underground realm, with its shut and carefully guarded little door, in the midst of Book II. He completes this latter task, first by rejecting the gold which he is told would gain him worldly honour (not, be it noted, sensual gratification, which belongs elsewhere), then by rejecting the struggle for high rank embodied in Philotime, and finally by rejecting what I take to be the ambition to surpass the human and put on the divine, in the Garden of Proserpina.

The most difficult of these points about the Cave of Mammon is probably the last, although what I have said about it is fairly close to Frank Kermode's well known essay.[12] The confluence of embodied traditions in the culminating episode of the Garden of Proserpina is so rich that it requires extensive discussion, although in a way this is a pity. The aesthetic and narrative success of this episode is at least in question. Nevertheless, with a poet like Spenser it is well worth while to get at the basis of his thinking even where he does not seem to some of us to have found an adequate embodiment for it. I shall return later to the more general matter of the representation of the two forms of intemperance throughout Book II.

Turning our attention now to the Cave of Mammon, the Garden of Proserpina, and everything in the latter's episodic context, we may first ask whether there is any preliminary useful parallel to draw with the central passages of I and III. Mammon says that he oversees the constant flowing forth of worldly goods from the bosom of the earth, where they are bred (II.vii.8). In much the same way Genius oversees the flowing forth, and the return, of beings who are bred up in his Garden of Adonis

(III.vi.32,33). But the difference between these two porters lies of course in their relation to Nature. That Genius is the servant or priest of Nature everyone knows, and this is emphasized by Spenser. Conversely, Guyon says of men's reception of Mammon's gifts: 'But would they thinke, with how small allowaunce / Untroubled Nature doth her selfe suffise, / Such superfluities they would despise' (II.vii.15). He continues with the Ovidian Golden Age, and then says that the pride of later ages exceeded 'naturall first need' (16). The unnatural torturing of the earth's minerals is of course a general feature of the Cave of Mammon, and the adversary character of the Garden of Proserpina to any garden or *locus amoenus* grown by course of kind, like the Garden of Adonis, is sufficiently obvious.

For purposes, now, of a direct attack upon the secrets of the Garden of Proserpina most of the earlier commentators – to mention such variously significant names as Hughes, Taine, Kate M. Warren, Padelford, Greenlaw – are not of much help, having largely ignored the episode. Some, like de Selincourt and Lotspeich, have found in it only a form of avarice or covetousness, as an extension of the earlier Mammon episodes, although they have not bothered to explain what this has to do with Pontius Pilate (stanza 62), for example. Still others see in it a form of pride, as an extension of the immediately preceding episode of Philotime, the love of worldly honour. Very recently a number of scholars have approached the questions of the Garden of Proserpina. Three of the longest and most systematic treatments of the matter belong to Harry Berger,[13] to Frank Kermode as mentioned, and to Paul Alpers.[14] I shall deal only briefly with Berger's theory, because all of the theories about a major shortcoming in Guyon's character or behaviour *as an individual* seem to me to lead into a blind alley. There may be a soft impeachment of priggishness in Guyon's being made to feed himself with comfort of his own virtues and praiseworthy deeds at II.vii.2; there may be a later reminder to Guyon that he cannot live by that bread alone. But even this is indistinct, and I shall leave out of court here, as so many others have recently done, the notion of Guyon's *particular* faultiness; his sin, as J.R.R. Tolkien said of Beowulf, is only that he is a member of the human race.

I do not share Alpers's disagreement with Kermode's subtle speculations about the Garden of Proserpina; in fact my position depends upon Kermode's in an important sense. I should also say that whatever the mistakes and improper emphases may be of the school edition of the first two books of *The Faerie Queene* by Professors Kellogg and Steele,[15] they have made some daring guesses about this episode which seem to me impressive. I make use of a number of them.

To return to Alpers, I find that his own interpretation of the Cave of Mammon is one of the less satisfying features of his important book, and that within the Cave of Mammon sequence, he has least to tell us about the Garden of Proserpina. Surely there is much in his treatment which points in the right direction: in general, we should read along the main, well known lines of mythological and iconographical tradition in the Renaissance, unless the pressure of Spenser's specific words takes us farther afield. Certainly the obvious ground-bass of cupidity and avarice plays straight through from the meeting with Mammon into the Garden itself. Certainly one of the commonsensical reasons for the appearance of Tantalus near the end of the Garden passage is that he has a reputation in the Renaissance for being a miser, from Boccaccio onward. Most important of all, in my estimation, is the notion that one of Guyon's early indignant replies to Mammon intimates part of the subsequent pattern of symbolism in the Garden: (II.vii.15,16)

> Indeede (quoth he) through fowle intemperaunce,
> > Frayle men are oft captiv'd to covetise:
> > But would they thinke, with how small allowaunce
> > Untroubled Nature doth her selfe suffise,
> > Such superfluities they would despise,
> > Which with sad cares empeach our native joyes:
> > At the well head the purest streames arise:
> But mucky filth his braunching armes annoyes,
> And with uncomely weedes the gentle wave accloyes.

> The antique world, in his first flowring youth,
> > Found no defect in his Creatours grace,
> > But with glad thankes, and unreproved truth,

The gifts of soveraigne bountie did embrace:
Like Angels life was then mens happy cace;
But later ages pride, like corn-fed steed,
Abusd her plenty, and fat swolne encreace
To all licentious lust, and gan exceed
The measure of her meane, and naturall first need.

But in spite of these points, to which Alpers has properly drawn our attention, one of the features of the Cave of Mammon sequence, as Kermode points out and as Alpers admits, is that the associations keep enriching themselves and the ideas keep ramifying, through the throne-room of Philotime, where the idea of worldly honour through meed (that is, *mede*, in the senses in which this word is used in *Piers Plowman*) is added to mere money-madness, and presumably on into the Garden of Proserpina.

One minor slip which, I consider, leads to a fallacious distinction in Alpers's interpretation can be soon disposed of. He tries to distinguish (p. 243) between the baleful vegetation at the beginning of the Garden passage, in stanzas 51 and 52, which he considers to be unambiguously evil and unnatural, and the tree with the golden fruit in the following stanzas, which he considers to be ambiguous in quality: it has, he says, both good and evil effects and speaks to us, thus, of the possibilities of choice in the heroic moral life. He begins the argument for this distinction by pointing to the adjective 'goodly': in stanza 53, line 6, 'Next thereunto did grow a *goodly* tree,' and in stanza 54, 'Their fruit were golden apples glistring bright, / That *goodly* was their glory to behold ...' He neglects to note, however, that the adverb 'goodly' is similarly applied to the fitting out of the garden with those same baleful plants that are indeed unrelievedly evil: in stanza 51, line 4, 'a gardin goodly garnished / With hearbs and fruits, whose kinds mote not be red ...,' and so on, into an enumeration. There is not really anything to choose between the earlier, black vegetation and the later, golden-fruited tree: it is only, as I hope to show, that the vegetation is an evidence of evil, while the apples are an allurement towards it.

There are a number of more important points where I find Alpers's interpretation less than satisfactory. One of them will do as an example: his treatment of Tantalus and Pilate floating with many more in the waters of Cocytus. Alpers has told us (page 261) that at the very simplest level of the Proserpina sequence we are dealing with riches and their abuse, but that beyond this we are made aware in these two figures of certain truths of the moral life and of moral heroism. Both Tantalus and Pilate have sadly come short of the moral imperative placed upon them as important men (pages 273–4).

One sees how this works in the case of Tantalus: as a rich man, he imitates the lavishness of Mammon in feasting the gods. He is guilty of ambitious self-assertion, through his great possessions. But how does this work for Pilate? He is indeed represented as guilty in having abdicated moral judgment: he has allowed Christ to be killed. But what does this have to do with Riches? There is no tradition in that direction, nor does Alpers claim one. He would perhaps say that my logical dilemma arises from an inflexible way of reading allegory, contrary to what Rosemond Tuve's *Allegorical Imagery*[16] has taught us. But with due respect to his instructive book this will not do. Whether we are talking about the allegorical tradition of the *Commedia*, or of the *Pèlerinage de la Vie Humaine*, or of the *Mirror for Magistrates*, the expectation would be the same: those two wallowing down there with many more in that feculent water should surely have more in common than a general lapse from the heroic – into lavishness in one case and pusillanimity in the other. They should *share* a specific sin, just as all those in the chamber of Philotime suffer from ambition. I am fairly sure that something else in common between these two figures and the Socrates who is an image in the Proserpina episode will show us part of Spenser's plan.

Why then, first, are those two together in Cocytus? We have already said that Tantalus is a miser, to be punished in the general context of the Cave. Another common-sense datum is that both Tantalus and Pilate may properly be submerged, because Tantalus is traditionally punished in this way, and because Pilate has in common with Lady Macbeth and with Ruddymane that his hands are traditionally, and often unavailingly, washed in water. But the common submersibility of these two characters is not enough of a common denominator. There should be some shared malefaction (involving intemperance, of course) between these two who are so obviously classed together.

Tantalus tries unsuccessfully to drink the filthy water and to reach the golden apples of Proserpina's tree: he suffers from thirst and hunger but cannot die. This is, of course, in large part the traditional punishment. But now consider what Spenser makes Tantalus, and then Guyon, say, beginning in stanza 59:

> Lo *Tantalus*, I here tormented lye:
> Of whom high *Jove* wont whylome feasted bee,
> Lo here I now for want of food doe dye:
> But if that thou be such, as I thee see,
> Of grace I pray thee, give to eat and drinke to mee.

> Nay, Nay, thou greedie *Tantalus* (quoth he)
> Abide the fortune of thy present fate,
> And unto all that live in high degree,
> Ensample be of mind intemperate,
> To teach them how to use their present state.
> Then gan the cursed wretch aloud to cry,
> Accusing highest *Jove* and gods ingrate,
> And eke blaspheming heaven bitterly,
> As authour of unjustice, there to let him dye.

Guyon calls Tantalus greedy and an example of intemperance of mind to those in high position, so that they will know better how to use their 'state' – both their place in life, in a hierarchy of rank, and the outward show which goes with this. It is certainly true that Spenser is talking about a kind of Lucullan ostentation here, as Alpers might maintain, but beyond the *magnificence* of the banquet there are more specific concerns. Three facts are emphasized: 1 / it was the highest of the gods whom he feasted; 2 / now he is so low that he cannot feed even himself; 3 / he believes that the gods owe him a living, because he thinks that he as a man has been able to do them favours.

On the basis of these statements I believe that we can satisfactorily explain Tantalus by means of the classical traditions, which knew little of his avarice. Spenser shows his acquaintance with one of these traditions in his other most extensive mention of Tantalus, in *Virgil's Gnat* 385–8, where Tantalus is punished because he 'did the bankets of the Gods bewray,' that is, he revealed the secrets of the gods' banquets. One thing that seems to be meant, then, is that the Tantalus of the Garden of Proserpina aspired to traffic with the gods – that he wished to commune with them on even terms in a way unsuitable to humankind, and banqueted them ostentatiously in order to do so. With his usual sangfroid Spenser has heightened the emphasis of the classical myth by making Tantalus the giver of the banquet. Certainly this interpretation of Tantalus's and Guyon's words is all that I need for the point which I have in mind here.

It is tempting, however (even if it is not necessary for the explanation which I propose), to go beyond the literal sense of these words to a possibility which has already been suggested by others.[17] Another and better known story about Tantalus's feasting than the one about the gods' secret counsels – one many times referred to in sixteenth-century English verse – is that Tantalus was punished for serving his son Pelops as a meal to the gods, an act which he had performed because he was ambitious to test their omniscience. As you know, only Pelops's shoulder was consumed, and only by the goddess Ceres, distracted by grief for her daughter, Proserpina. It is interesting and perhaps significant that Tantalus's punishment should now be transferred by Spenser to the edge of Proserpina's garden. A final reason for this more radical interpretation has to do with thematic symmetry: that is, a parallel to the Infernal journey of Duessa in Book i. Duessa is mainly concerned there to find Aesculapius so as to cure Sansjoy. Aesculapius, we learn at some length, had been hurled into hell because Jove feared a human's attainment of divine abilities. Aesculapius had demonstrated these abilities by reintegrating Hippolytus, who had been torn into pieces at his father's request. A pattern, then, according to which one character – Tantalus – is punished for seeking traffic with the divine by dismembering his son who is then revived, and according to which in the second place another character – Aesculapius – is punished for his display of apparently divine powers by which he had reassembled and revived a youth torn to pieces at the request of his father, sounds attractively like that of a sixteenth-century exegete. But I do not claim complete demonstration. The pattern sounds like that of a twentieth-century exegete as well.

Concerning Tantalus's fellow in punishment, Pilate, we hear that he is washing his hands in the filthy water, through which they become only more dirty. We may say here in passing, so as to dispose of the point, that Guyon's earlier statement to Mammon is now borne out: (ii.vii.15)

> At the well head the purest streames arise:
> But mucky filth his braunching armes annoyes,
> And with uncomely weedes the gentle wave accloyes,

with the addition in the next stanza concerning later, more sophisticated, races' not being satisfied with our 'creatours grace.' Neither Ruddymane's nor Pilate's hands may be cleaned, but Ruddymane is in his proper person guiltless, and is washed in the pure well of a fountain of chastity, flowing forth from a nymph who had died to preserve this virtue (ii.ii.1–10) under the favour of Diana. It is interesting, too, to compare this well with that in the central passage of Book i, the well whose nymph is out of Diana's favour, and which is associated with Redcross's unchastity.

To continue, however, with Pilate. He describes himself, not as Tantalus has done, as a victim of injustice, but as an agent of it:

> I *Pilate* am the falsest Judge, alas,
> And most unjust, that by unrighteous
> And wicked doome, to Jewes despiteous
> Delivered up the Lord of life to die,
> And did acquite a murdrer felonous;
> The whiles my hands I washt in puritie,
> The whiles my soule was soyld with foule iniquitie.

What, now, may we say that Tantalus and Pilate have in common, when we consider all the pressures and changes of focus in these lines concerning them, and when we remember that we are in the context of the central episode of Book ii, quite possibly as centrally significant as the parallel passages in Books i and iii? It seems to me that the proper answer is man's infringement upon, and arrogation of, the divine – Satanic and intemperate pride. But before we step back and consider the appropriateness of this to its larger context, let us consider the first exemplum in the section of canto vii devoted to the Garden of Proserpina. In stanza 51 the herbs and fruits are generally mentioned, and in stanza 52 there is an enumeration of poisonous plants, with a final, single exemplary reference:

> There mournfull *Cypresse* grew in greatest store,
> And trees of bitter *Gall*, and *Heben* sad,
> Dead sleeping *Poppy*, and blacke *Hellebore*,
> Cold *Coloquintida*, and *Tetra* mad,
> Mortall *Samnitis*, and *Cicuta* bad,
> With which th'unjust *Atheniens* made to dy
> Wise *Socrates*, who thereof quaffing glad
> Pourd out his life, and last Philosophy
> To the faire *Critias* his dearest Belamy.

Certainly Spenser is not following the standard account of Socrates' death in the *Phaedo*, because Critias is not mentioned there, and, while he was once the associate, he was certainly no belamy of Socrates. What I believe has really happened here was set forth long ago, by Upton.[18] Xenophon tells in the *Hellenica* (II.iii.15) that the Athenian Theramenes had Critias as friend (φίλος here being susceptible to, although not requiring, the interpretation borne in Spenser's passage by the Chaucerian word *belamy*, applied in *The Canterbury Tales* by the Host to the Pardoner).[19] Critias, however, as one of the Thirty Tyrants, had Theramenes unjustly condemned to death by poison. Theramenes then drank the poison, saying with what is likely to have been ironical intent in the context in the *Hellenica*. 'To the health of *fair* Critias' (or 'beautiful,' or 'handsome, Critias') (II.iii.56).

Spenser has substituted Socrates for Theramenes and has given to Critias the somewhat epicene character of some of the Platonic Socrates' interlocutors. He may have been led in the direction of this substitution, as Upton pointed out, by Cicero's telling of the story in the *Disputationes tusculanae* (I.xi), where, however, Critias is not said to be the friend of Theramenes. After relating Xenophon's story, Cicero draws an explicit parallel with the case of Socrates: he says (and I translate), 'After a few years Socrates went into the same prison and partook of the same goblet, by the same kind of miscarriage of justice,' and then Cicero equates Theramenes and Socrates as men famous for virtue and wisdom. Spenser has conflated the two stories and given an affective colouring to the friendship. That *belamy* gives a *literal* translation of the adjectives used by Xenophon and Cicero seems to me to clinch Upton's case here, although it is true that Spenser seems confused about Critias in a slightly different way at one other point in *The Faerie Queene* (iv.Prologue.3). But why should he have conflated the accounts in this one spot, as no one else has done, so far as we know? Why would not Socrates drinking the poison without reference to a supposed cruel beloved have done just as well? A satisfactory explanation is at hand if we assume that Spenser needed a third myth of the selfish, egotistical human profanation of the divine by the merely creaturely. As we know, it is a commonplace of much Renaissance Platonizing thought, including Ficino's, that Socrates is a type of Christ, or a 'first Christ' – a man who, as the first Platonist, directly intellected the one, the true, and the good; offered, by his teaching and his life, an ideal to his people; and by them was unjustly, but judicially, condemned to death. The passages concerning Socrates and Christ are strikingly parallel: In stanza 52, 'Th'unjust *Atheniens* made to dy / Wise Socrates'; in stanza 62, '... the falsest Judge, alas, / And most unjust, that by unrighteous / And wicked doome, to Jewes despiteous / Delivered up the Lord of life to die.' In the case of Socrates, then, the Athenians, urged on by Socrates' dearly loved friend, condemned and destroyed a type of Christ, who had their interests at heart and to whom they ought to have been devoted. In the case of Pilate, the Son of Man, the physical embodiment of the Godhead, who loves us and whom we ought to love, was condemned to the mortal judgment of his people, and a guilty man was pardoned in his place; in the case of Tantalus, a human intemperately sought commerce with the gods, or, possibly we may say that a son, whom Tantalus ought to have loved in particular, was sacrificed for a meal for the gods, so that the unnatural and impious father might test their knowledge. I do not wish to push the analogy of sacrificial meals and rebirth, or indeed the whole matter of Pelops, but the vindication and rebirth of both the latter victims may be noted.

I should like to stress how elegantly and exactly this interpretation fits the context of cantos vii and viii. Around the throne of Philotime, with its golden chain reaching towards heaven, we have seen the aspiration to worldly glory. Guyon's final reaction to Philotime is that he, 'fraile flesh and earthly wight,' is 'Unworthy match for such immortall mate,' and with the next episode, the Garden of Proserpina, we approach the most intemperate of all human aspirations, that towards the divine. In the begining of canto viii the pathos of God's love and grace for man is emphasized by what is now promised in response to what had formerly been acted out:

> But O th' exceeding grace
> Of highest God, that loves his creatures so,
> And all his workes with mercy doth embrace,
> That blessed Angels, he sends to and fro,
> To serve to wicked man, to serve his wicked foe.
>
> How oft do they, their silver bowers leave,
> To come to succour us, that succour want?
> How oft do they with golden pineons, cleave
> The flitting skyes, like flying Pursuivant,
> Against foule feends to aide us millitant?

It seems to me that the choice of the unaccustomed adjective 'silver' to characterize the bowers from which the divine messengers come is largely dictated by the *silver seat* of the divinity Proserpina in the preceding canto, which Guyon has refused to occupy. Not for him is the sitting in divine seats and banqueting on unsuitable viands which are within the mana of the divine. The silver seat is of course the same one in which Theseus presumptuously sat and was imprisoned, but Theseus ate no golden apples. Spenser is again conflating: in a general sense, the eating of fruit was what condemned Proserpina to stay in the Lower Regions; no doubt the fact that the fruit of the tree is an apple, too, has Edenic significance, but where Kermode thought that the apples were there to tempt us to forbidden knowledge, *scientes bonum et malum*, I suggest that the temptation involves the other half of Satan's promise to Eve: the promise of a forbidden role: *Eritis sicut dii.*

I cannot follow Kermode, then, into the precisely Miltonic atmosphere of the Serpent's temptation of Eve to divine sapience alone, but the context remains strikingly Miltonic in any case. It was not for nothing that Milton commented so attentively on the Cave of Mammon episodes, which teach 'us to see, and know, and yet abstain.' His chief non-abstainer, Eve, is moved at the last minute by her growing hunger and the deliciousness of the fruit: (*PL* ix.739–43)

> Meanwhile the hour of Noon drew on, and wak'd
> An eager appetite, rais'd by the smell
> So savory of that Fruit, which with desire,
> Inclinable now grown to touch or taste,
> Solicited her longing eye ...

Similarly, Guyon's hunger and exhaustion, described in stanza 65 ('want of food, and sleepe, which two upbeare, / Like mightie pillours, this fraile life of man,'), were already operative a little before when he, or the reader, was exposed to so many mentions of eating, drinking, and rest: Socrates drinks; Proserpina is described as habitually resting in the shade; the edible fruit of the tree appear; Tantalus feasted the gods, and now demands food and drink; finally Guyon himself is tempted to rest in the cool of the shaded seat and to eat a golden apple. It needs only to be added that Guyon, like Milton's great abstainer, comes through his long temptations triumphantly and is angelically ministered to. His imitation of the divine is licit, unlike all the others.

We have now attempted an explanation of three situations – those involving Socrates and Critias, Tantalus and possibly but not surely Pelops, Pilate and Christ. What remains of the episode of the Garden of Proserpina are the exempla in stanzas 54 and 55 of Hercules, Atalanta, Acontius, and Paris. I suspect that it is here that Alpers might most likely accuse me, as he did Kermode, of tailoring the text to fit one's own interpretation, but perhaps in my case he would have started making the accusation earlier than this. He suggests that the only common traits of these exempla are that they have to do with gold and that they instruct us in the equivocal character of the heroic life of accomplishment. Perhaps so, but in the context of fruit which has tempted one female, Proserpina, so that she is held in the Lower Regions, and which prefigures the temptation of another woman, Eve, it seems that the temptation of yet two other women in two of these exempla is likely to belong within the same set of ideas. What is probably the best known mediaeval telling of the exemplum of Atalanta, in the *Gesta Romanorum*, is moralized in such a way that the lover who dropped the three successive golden apples – those, as Spenser says in stanza 54, 'with which th'*Euboean* young man wan / Swift *Atalanta*, when through craft he her out ran,' dropping them before her in the midst of her race – is the devil tempting the human soul. It is very likely, of course, that this much-beloved compilation was known to Spenser.[20] The first 'history' in the sixteenth-century English version concerns 'a mighty Emperour which had a fayre creature to his Daughter, named Athalanta ...' The story continues in the usual way. The successful lover is named 'Pomeis' ('Pomeys' in Wynkyn de Worde), presumably because of his connection with apples. He provides himself with 'three bals of Gold against the running' (not described as apples, however, in the story) and proceeds in the usual way. The 'morall' at the end of the history reads in part thus:

> By this Emperour is understood the Father of heaven, and
> by the Damsell is understood the Soule of man, with whom
> many Divels desire to run, and to deceive her through their
> temptaciouns, but she withstandeth them mightily, and
> overcommeth them. And when they have done their worst,
> and may not speede, then maketh he three bals of gold,
> and casteth them before her in the three ages of man, that
> is to say, in youth, in manhood, and in old age. In youth
> the Divell casteth the ball of Lecherie before her, that is to
> say, desire of the flesh ... The second ball is the ball of pride,
> that which the Divell casteth to man in his manhood ... the
> third ball ... is Covetousnesse, that the Divell casteth to
> man in his old age ...

I conclude, therefore, that the references to Atalanta and also to the 'lover trew' of Acontius[21] in stanzas 54 and 55 of the

Garden episode are further orchestrations of the theme of successful temptations of females by fruit, a theme which begins with Eve's implanted wish to be as gods, so contrary to the temperance of Guyon and of Christ when exposed to similar blandishments.

To speak now of the rest of the exempla in these stanzas, the instance of Hercules and the taking of the golden apples of the Hesperides from the daughters of Atlas may be no more than an origin-myth encouraged by a similarity of names. As Spenser says, these apples do indeed originate from beneath the earth, for the apples of the Hesperides were a present from Earth to Hera when she married Zeus. These apples of the daughters of *Atlas* which Hercules seized were supposed by Natalis Comes to be the source of the ones with which *Atalanta* was finally overcome. I incline to the view, however, that this episode, together with the final one of the Judgment of Paris, involves an instance of presumption against the divine, with the baleful consequence in the latter case, 'That many noble *Greekes* and *Troians* made to bleed' – a consequence so important that it forms the backdrop for the earliest heroic poem known to Spenser, in which the gods intimately involve themselves with humans.

In summary, what I have to offer thus far is the following. The Garden of Proserpina continues the representation of the intemperance of avarice, as do the other episodes connected with Mammon, through the symbolism of golden apples, a silver seat, and the figure of the Renaissance Tantalus. But after the intemperate desire for worldly honour centred in the throne and chain of Philotime, the Garden proper extends the concepts of prideful possession of money and what it buys, and of quickly won lofty status in the world, to the final intemperance of human desire for or infringement upon the realm of the divine. An exemplum of the selfish destruction, by his imagined beloved, of Socrates, a type of the divine, begins the episode; it is ended with Pilate's *mea culpa* for the monstrous sacrifice of God by the world which he loves. In the figure of Tantalus are focused, along with his avarice, the desire to test the gods, possibly the unauthorized sacrifice of his son to attain his wish, an egotistical resentment against them, and a punishment which, possibly in its location and certainly in its nature, is proper to him. He is punished at the shore of the island of Proserpina, who is the daughter of the deity whom, possibly, he had succeeded in particularly offending, because that mother was rendered defenseless by concern for Proserpina herself. Extreme hunger is the nature of his punishment, and so it should be for an ostentatious banqueter of whom it may possibly be said that he had given his son as a meal to the gods; hunger, in any case, is the chief vehicle for the motif of temptation in the Garden. He is a very useful symbol in Spenser's pattern, because in him the desires for gold, divinity, and nourishment converge. By the chair which it is death to sit in, we are reminded of Theseus' daring presumption against the Infernal gods. By the apples of Proserpina's tree, and by Mammon's invitation to Guyon to eat of them, we are reminded of the primal temptation of Eve by Satan to be as a god, and of her succumbing to this sin. Such temptation of a woman, and her yielding, are repeated in the motif, implicit here, of Proserpina's eating of fruit and being thus compelled to remain in Hades, and in the successful use of golden apples to enthral Atalanta and the beloved of Acontius. Hercules' seizing of the golden apples from the daughters of Atlas may simply explain the source of the apples to seduce Atalanta, or it may be another case of presumption against the divine. Paris's unavoidable meddling with divinities at odds with each other over a golden apple is another such instance; it led to the greatest tragedy of classical myth and of the archetypal heroic poem: the Trojan War.

The repeated motifs of temptation so far are, of course, a continuation of a theme current throughout the Cave of Mammon sequence, but the many images of nourishment in which these temptations take form are attuned to Guyon's now nearly exhausted state. That Guyon should have resisted the temptation to assume the trappings of divinity, even though the apple would have eased his hunger and the seat would have relieved his fatigue, dissociates him from Eve and the others, and makes him a close imitator of every Christian's model, Christ himself, who, hungry and fatigued in the desert, yet rejected the temptation to assume the prerogatives of his godhead and relieve his hunger, and, a second Adam, abstained where Adam fell. In consequence, Guyon is angelically ministered to, as was Christ.[22] For humankind as such, this is an instance of God's unquenchable grace. That Guyon is not divine, but merely human, is no more a reproach to him than it is to Beowulf in his mortal dragon-fight. Strong beyond most men, he yet faints, and the exceeding of his vital powers only confirms that all of us, sons of Adam, are finally open to the kinds of intemperance represented by Pyrochles and Cymochles – loss of control, loss of direction. Even so, he is saved from them by a vessel of divine aid, Arthur. Guyon's rebuff to those who infringe upon the divine, his refusal of the golden apple and the silver seat, and his being subsequently ministered to correspond well with what we are told in the Sermon on the Mount, as it appears in the Gospel for the fifteenth Sunday after Trinity in the Second Prayer-Book of Edward VI:

> ... ye canne not serve God and Mammon. Therefore I saye unto you; be not carefull for your lyfe, what ye shall eate or dryncke: nor yet for your body, what rayments ye shall put on ... Therefore, take no thought, saying: what shall we eate, or what shal we drinke, or wherwith shall we be clothed? after all these thynges do the Gentyles seke. For youre heavenly father knoweth that ye have nede of all these thynges. But rather seeke ye first the kyngdome of god, and the righteousness thereof, and all these thynges shal be ministered unto you.

We may now deal with the possibilities of further points of symbolic contact opened up by this interpretation of the Garden of Proserpina and by the numerical parallel between the centre-points of the first three books. I should like to take up some less important resemblances first.

A general line of symbolic and moral parallelism between Book II and Book I is fairly obvious: the temptations through bodily hunger and through satanic ambition, in the centre of the Book of Temperance, to infringe upon the realm that is not properly ours, are paralleled in the centre of the Book of Holiness by a temptation of a more cunning duplicity – Duessa's, like that of a disguised Vice in a Morality – to forsake purity and oneness, and to enter upon the pride of the flesh.

Certain symbolic symmetries between Book II and Book III are less obvious. We earlier made the points that both Mammon and Genius are in some sense porters superintending a constant flow from the earth, and that the unnatural in Mammon's realm faces the natural character of Genius's, in a very familiar way. But it is tempting to go beyond this. One lead of which I can make very little is that in Spenser's most revered English predecessor Proserpina is a 'Quene of Fayerye,'[23] in *The Merchant's Tale* – 'the fairy queen Proserpina' is what Thomas Campion later calls her.[24] Perhaps Proserpina as an Infernal counterpart of the true Faerie Queene, Gloriana, is worth thinking about; this would count somewhat for Alpers' case about the choices of the heroic moral life, although it will not get us very far with parallels to the centre of Book III. What does seem relevant in that regard is that Spenser knew both Proserpina and Adonis as seasonal deities: Proserpina, having eaten half the seeds of the pomegranate, stays in the Lower Regions in the cold half of the year, but joins her mother Ceres to restore vegetation on earth in the spring. Adonis, killed by the boar, is reborn; and with him vegetation springs up again. It is tempting to develop our own fertility myth here, and to say that the Garden of Proserpina is, archetypically speaking, the season of death and sterility, within which are concealed certain promises of rebirth (did not both Christ and Pelops rise again?); and that the Garden of Adonis displays the actuality of an eternal rebirth. But, with all respect to A.C. Hamilton and Northrop Frye, I am not sure that this was Spenser's matured plan. The sterility and unnaturalness of Proserpina's Garden ought to be just that and nothing more within the moral plan of the career of Guyon in Book II. Some such idea, however, may have been the one with which Spenser started.[25]

I want to close, now, with what I take to be my two most important points concerning the structure of Book II, and the structure of the three-book edition of 1590.

As I have already said, the two opposite forms which intemperance takes in Book II at large are concupiscible slackness and irascible contention. To describe the sensual abandon of Mordant and the suicide of Amavia in canto i we have the initial statement of this division, quoted earlier. We have said or implied that Perissa and Sansloy are concupiscibly loose; Elissa and Huddibras, irascibly contentious. Cymochles and Pyrochles are similarly differentiated, by act as well as by etymology. The two helpers of Maleger in his battle with Arthur are Impotence and Impatience. The twin dangers for the temperance of Guyon humself are described in such terms as 'weake fleshlinesse' and 'strong passion' (ii.iv.2).

My most general contention concerning Book ii is that, as Guyon defeats the first of these forms of intemperance – concupiscible slackness – at the end of Book ii in the Bower of Bliss, so also he deals with the advanced forms of the second – irascible contentiousness – in the middle of Book ii in his Infernal journey with Mammon, culminating in the Garden of Proserpina. The whole of this latter sequence contains no example of the specifically concupiscible or carnal. Hell, divided from the 'house of Richesse' by 'but a litle stride,' shows personifications of Revenge, Despite, Treason, Hate, Jealousy, Fear, Sorrow, Shame, Horror, which might all be described as belonging to the Amavia-Pyrochles-Atin-Impatience axis. By contrast, in Book i the first mentioned citizen of hell in Duessa's Infernal journey is a sufferer for carnality: '*Ixion* turned on a wheele, / For daring tempt the Queene of heaven to sin' (v.35). Money is not recommended by Mammon in Book ii, or blamed by Guyon, for its ability to attract and hold beauty – what Sir Epicure Mammon mainly saw in it. Rather, it has to do with contention and anger. Guyon looks upon the effects of wealth not as debauchery, but as (ii.vii.12.7,8)

Strife, and debate, bloudshed, and bitternesse,
Outrageous wrong, and hellish covetize.

Our first introduction to Mammon is to a scornful god: 'Thereat with staring eyes fixed askance, / In great disdaine, he answerd ...' (vii. 7. 5,6). And the porter of Philotime's throne room is himself Disdayne (41). Philotime has, says Mammon, been thrust out by the gods for envy (49). Upon her chain of Ambition, all 'thought to raise themselves to high degree,' 'But every one did strive his fellow downe to throw' (47). Contention again.

Guyon's humble declaration, when offered Philotime, that he is 'Unworthy match for such immortall mate,' is, as we have noticed, a proper introduction to Mammon's irate conducting of him into the Garden of Proserpina in the next stanza. There I have already tried to convince you that human infringement upon the divine, and the temptation in this direction, are the main themes: certainly these are cases of contentious striving. Tantalus, who receives much fuller treatment than any of the other subjects here, is as irascible as possible: this is yet one more of the symbolic lines which focus in his person. Perhaps more importantly, he and Pilate, the other chief figure treated, share a trait with other irascibly contentious characters in Book II: they seek to still their need in water.

The entrances to the House of Mammon and the Bower of Bliss stand in striking contrast. Of Mammon conducting Guyon we are told in canto vii, stanza 24, line 5 'At last him to a litle dore he brought': (vii.25,26)

> Before the dore sat selfe-consuming Care,
>   Day and night keeping wary watch and ward,
>   For feare least Force or Fraud should unaware
>   Breake in, and spoile the treasure there in gard ...

> So soone as *Mammon* there arriv'd, the dore
>   To him did open, and affoorded way;
>   Him followed eke Sir *Guyon* evermore,
>   Ne darkenesse him, ne daunger might dismay.
>   Soone as he entred was, the dore streight way
>   Did shut, and from behind it forth there lept
>   An ugly feend, more fowle than dismall day,
>   The which with monstrous stalke behind him stept,
> And ever as he went, dew watch upon him kept.

On the other hand, we hear of the Bower as Guyon and the Palmer confront it that its fence was 'but weake and thin; / Nought feard their force, that fortilage to win ... And eke the gate was wrought of substaunce light, / Rather for pleasure, than for battery or fight' (xii.43). Further, the gate (xii.46)

ever open stood to all,
Which thither came: but in the Porch there sate
A comely personage of stature tall,
And semblaunce pleasing, more than naturall,
That travellers to him seemd to entize;
His looser garment to the ground did fall,
And flew about his heeles in wanton wize,
Not fit for speedy pace, or manly exercize.

The gates, the attitudes towards forceful interlopers, and the
guardians stand in what seems to me to be a planned relationship
of opposition to each other. Also, completely congruent with the
notion that Guyon's chief victories over the two forms of intem-
perance occur in the Cave of Mammon and in the Bower of Bliss
is Spenser's somewhat curious contention that the two chief
villains to lay siege to the noblest of Alma's senses, that of the
sight, are 'Beautie, and money' (xi.9). Finally, and perhaps most
significantly, as the most virulent intemperance of the Cave of
Mammon is the human aspiration to rise to the level of the divine,
so that of the Bower of Bliss is the descent in the hierarchy to
the merely animal: Tantalus and Grill stand at opposite extremes
from the temperately human (see vii.60 and xii.87).

It is true, of course, that at the end of the Cave of Mammon
sequence there is added to the chief temptation of disdainful
ambition the subsidiary one of a kind of sensual gratification:
the golden apples, which embody ambition, are also supposed to
taste good; and the silver chair, which it is overweening to sit
in, might also offer comfort to Guyon's weary shanks. Sensual
gratification similar to this will be offered to Guyon as he *enters*
the Bower of Bliss. Similarly, the Bower of Bliss, which is pri-
marily devoted to sensual impotence, is indirectly related to
'smart' – the pain of violent impatience – for Mordant's sensual
gratification with Acrasia, which led to his death when water met
the draught that he had already drunk, in turn led to Amavia's
fatal stabbing of herself and to the blood-curdling fate of Ruddy-
mane, dabbling his hands in his mother's blood. In fact the wish
for a symbolic coincidence is what probably led Spenser to sub-
stitute, in the art-work on the gate of the Bower, the violent story
of Jason and Medea in place of Tasso's familiar stories of Her-

cules and Iole, Antony and Cleopatra, in a passage otherwise
very strongly imitative of the *Gerusalemme Liberata* (in which
see especially XVI.3–7). On this gate Medea is seen to throw the
bloody pieces of her brother's body into the sea so as to delay
her father's pursuit of her and Jason, caught in their mutual
infatuation; then we are shown Medea's later murder by fire
of the Corinthian rival for Jason's affection and hand: (II.xii.45)

> Ye might have seene the frothy billowes fry
>   Under the ship, as thorough them she went,
>   That seemd the waves were into yvory,
>   Or yvory into the waves were sent;
>   And other where the snowy substaunce sprent
>   With vermell, like the boyes bloud therein shed,
>   A piteous spectacle did represent,
>   And otherwhiles with gold besprinkeled;
> Yt seemed th'enchaunted flame, which did *Creüsa* wed.

In the stanza showing the baby Ruddymane dabbling his hands
in the gore of his mother, who was, like Creusa, a victim of the
vengeance of a strong-willed competitor for a man's affections,
we have a similar blending of blood and water: (II.i.40)

> Pittifull spectacle of deadly smart,
>   Beside a bubbling fountaine low she lay,
>   Which she increased with her bleeding hart,
>   And the cleane waves with purple gore did ray;
>   Als in her lap a lovely babe did play
>   His cruell sport, in stead of sorrow dew;
>   For in her streaming blood he did embay
>   His litle hands, and tender joynts embrew;
> Pitifull spectacle, as ever eye did view.

The agreement of the phrases 'piteous spectacle' and the repeated
'Pittifull spectacle' should be noted.

In fact, to follow a side-issue for a moment, the pointing
through equivalent images in Book II is remarkable: Mordant
dies by water, Cymochles has water in his name, Pyrochles, burn-
ing, casts himself into water, Impatience drowns herself, Ruddy-

mane's bloody hands cannot be cleaned in pure water, Pilate (trying to wash his hands) and Tantalus float in a filthy river. Creusa dies by fire, Impatience is armed with flame, Mammon's helpers work with fire, Pyrochles has fire in his name. Amavia and Impotence both stab themselves.

But to return to the point: although Mammon finally mobilizes sensual appeals, and Acrasia falls to violent contention, the main direction of each of their two rules is now, I think, obvious.

My most general claim concerning the 1590 edition of *The Faerie Queene* is, finally, that in Book I we are given the defeat of Redcross 'in the middest' and his victory at the end; that in Book II we see the victory of Guyon over one of the chief forms of intemperance in the central episode, and over the other in the final episode; and that in Book III we are shown the perfection of chaste affection in the centre, but at the beginning and the end the degenerated form of that love in mastery, for which the cure will be *amicitia*, as shown in Britomart, in the 1590 conclusion of Book III, throughout the forthcoming Book IV of Friendship, and in the Isle of Venus of that book.

So that, finally, the arithmetical architecture of the first three books is put to work thus: in Book I, to project first failure and then victory; in Book II, to project the two extremes of which temperance is the mean; in Book III, to project the perfection and kindly import of enacted erotic pleasure, and the pain which is an aspect of *amor* if it is not complemented by the *amicitia* of which the conclusion of the third book in 1590 gives us a foretaste, to be continued in the future Book IV.[26]

NOTES

1 '*Amoretti* and the Dolce Stil Nuovo,' English 4, Modern Language Association Meeting, December 1968. This paper is scheduled to appear as an article in *English Literary Renaissance*.
2 In *Short Time's Endless Monument* (New York, 1960); reprinted by the Kennikat Press, 1972.
3 *Notes and Queries* 16 n.s. (January 1969), 24–6.
4 *Silent Poetry* (London, 1970). Dunlop's essay, 'The Unity of Spenser's *Amoretti*,' occupies pp. 153–69.

5   'Spenser's Timely Numbers: the Tally to Date,' English 4, Modern Language Association Meeting, December 1969; 'A Numerical Key for Spenser's *Amoretti* ... ,' *Yearbook of English Studies* 5 (1973).

6   Michael Baybak, Paul Delany, and A. Kent Hieatt, 'Placement "in the Middest" in *The Faerie Queene*,' *Papers on Languages & Literature* 5 (1969), 227–34.

7   (London, 1964).

8   Pp. 141–52.

9   All quotations of Spenser are from the Variorum edition, *The Works of Edmund Spenser* (Baltimore, 1932–49), with modernization of *i, u,* and *v*.

10 *Spenser and the Numbers of Time* (London, 1964), p. 40. The objection that the total line-count of 1590 is 17,999 instead of 18,000 does not convince me, because the 'silent' line in question, as Fowler points out, seems to be a conceit on Fidelia's stopping of the movement of the sun. This is in I.x.20, a stanza printed with only eight lines.

11 *The Enchanted Palace: Some Structural Aspects of 'Paradise Lost'* (Stockholm, 1967). See also William B. Hunter, 'The Center of *Paradise . Lost*,' *English Language Notes* 7 (1969), 32–4.

12 'The Cave of Mammon,' in *Elizabethan Poetry*, Stratford-upon-Avon Studies 2, ed. J.R. Brown and B. Harris (London, 1960).

13 *The Allegorical Temper: Vision and Reality in Book II of Spenser's 'Faerie Queene'* (New Haven, 1957).

14 *The Poetry of 'The Faerie Queene'* (Princeton, 1967), chap. 8. Since the preparation of the present essay another study has been published: Patrick Cullen, 'Guyon *Microchristus*: The Cave of Mammon Re-examined,' *ELH* 37 (1970), 153–74. This is a careful and full treatment with which I find myself in agreement at many points. I have summarized its argument in *Spenser Newsletter* 1:3 (Fall 1970), 9.

15 Edmund Spenser, *Books I and II of 'The Faerie Queene,' The Mutability Cantos and Selections from the Minor Poetry*, ed. Robert Kellogg and Oliver Steele (New York, 1965).

16 (Princeton, 1966).

17 Kellogg and Steele, eds., p. 315n.

18 *Variorum Spenser*, II, 263. I am indebted to my colleague Professor A.E. Raymond for his help with the problem of Theramenes, although the opinions here are entirely my own.

19 The introduction to *The Pardoner's Tale*, l. 318, in *The Works of Geoffrey Chaucer*, ed. F.N. Robinson (Boston, 1961), p. 148.

20 In either Latin or English. According to S.J. Herrtage, in the EETS edition (e.s. 33, 1879), an English edition was published by Wynkyn de Worde between 1510 and 1515. Herrtage cites testimony for seven more editions before 1602. STC lists one in 1557 and a number from 1595 onwards. In the Wynkyn de Worde edition, parts of which are reprinted by Herrtage, the first story is the one of Atalanta. It corresponds in all important respects to the one in the Folger Library copy of an edition of 1610 (1609 Old Style), which exists in the collection University Microfilms Early English Books, 1475–1640, Reel 648, which is the text used here.

21 The story of Acontius in the *Heroides* (20,21) is that his beloved
    Cydippe, while within the fane of the temple of Artemis, was per-
    suaded to read out loud the inscription on an apple, saying 'I swear by
    Artemis that I will marry none but Acontius,' and that she was then
    compelled by the goddess actually to marry him. With Spenser's words
    ('that goodly golden fruit, / With which *Acontius* got his lover trew,
    / Whom he had long time sought with fruitlesse suit ...') compare
    Milton's speech of Eve to her tempter: 'Serpent, we might have spar'd
    our coming hither, / Fruitless to mee, though Fruit be here to excess
    ...' (*PL* ix.647–8).
22 Dunlop holds that the middle 47 sonnets of *Amoretti* correspond to
    the period of Lent (46 days) and Easter Sunday. His argument makes
    this very difficult to deny. But a refinement of this, which I will
    attempt to justify in a forthcoming article, is that the 47 sonnets must
    be divided (at the sonnet corresponding to Lady Day or the beginning
    of the new year) into an earlier group of 40 sonnets (corresponding to
    the 40 days of Lent proper without its festive Sundays, which period
    of 40 days is based on the tradition of Christ's fast and suffering for
    40 days in the wilderness) and a later group of 7 sonnets (correspond-
    ing to those Sundays and to Easter). One reason for this division is
    that the mood changes to satisfaction at having gained the grace of the
    lady precisely at sonnet 62, the fortieth in the series. Now, the earlier
    denial of the lady's favour in the sonnet-sequence is to be thought of
    as Lenten only in terms of the season; Guyon's refusal to succumb to
    temptation is on the other hand a direct imitation of Christ. Yet I
    think that Spenser's mind was moving in the same channels in both
    cases. From Guyon's entrance into Mammon's House through its little
    door in stanza 26, up to his release in stanza 66, 40 stanzas intervene.
    Further, among the directly following stanzas in the succeeding canto
    (viii) there are resemblances to the group of seven sonnets in
    Amoretti. Particularly Sonnet 66, concerned with the heaven-sent
    qualities of the beloved to which the only exception is that she loves
    'so meane a one' as the poet, has much in common with the two
    stanzas, quoted above, which begin canto viii. For an additional and
    complementary pattern of 47 sonnets centred among all the stanzaic
    units of *Amoretti-Epithalamion*, see Alastair Fowler, *Triumphal
    Forms: Structural Patterns in Elizabethan Poetry* (Cambridge, 1970),
    pp. 180–2.
23 L. 2316, in *Works of Geoffrey Chaucer*, ed. Robinson, p. 125.
24 In the air beginning 'Hark, all you ladies that do sleep.'
25 One ought to cite here the case of Arethusa, parallel to that of
    Proserpina and told (in *Metamorphoses* v.527–641) to Ceres, who has
    just recovered her daughter. Arethusa had previously loved the hunt:
    she was a devotee of Diana. One day, wearied with the chase and
    pausing, so to speak, 'in middest of the race,' she had returned and
    bathed in the river Alpheus. At the last minute, in response to her
    chaste prayer, she was transformed by Diana into a stream, with
    which Alpheus, now again a river, then tried to mingle his waters.
    Diana opened a path to the Lower Regions, into which the stream

Arethusa flowed (we learn in another passage that she saw Proserpina there, and could report on her [487ff.]). Although Arethusa was thus swallowed up in darkness and apparently lost forever, yet she rose again into the light, as a fountain, in Ortygia, as Milton of course knew.

26 Probably I should note that the title of this paper indicates no desire to outgo either the poet Blake or Professor Frye. I called these symmetries 'fearful' only because they seemed to have remained in hiding for so long.

Emanations of glory:
Neoplatonic order in Spenser's *Faerie Queen*

ALASTAIR FOWLER

Not long ago it might have been considered quixotic to defend the order or unity of Spenser's incomplete masterpiece, which Derek Traversi could describe almost in an eighteenth-century manner as the poetic equivalent of a rambling badly ruined Gothic cathedral.[1] But Elizabethan art is less likely now to seem degenerate Gothic. We think we have a clearer idea of late Renaissance mannerism, a style characterized by complication, by avoidance of dominating focus, and by an almost Neogothic stylishness.[2] To risk another interart analogy, we would be inclined to compare *The Faerie Queen* to a *palazzo* of the *cinquecento* – or perhaps to a programmatic painting, filled with human figures, mythological deities, emblematic staffage, and subsidiary scenes in sequence and foreground-background relation. No one objects that Bloemart's *Banquet of the Gods* has too many figures, or that Titian's *Bacchus and Ariadne* lacks a single action. Mythological paintings, as Professor Wind has taught us to see, sometimes had a Neoplatonic significance; and so it is with Spenser's poem.

Here I should explain that I shall make no consistent attempt to distinguish 'orthodox' Renaissance Neoplatonism from the more diffuse Neoplatonism that had been assimilated to Christian and even perhaps to Judaic thought forms at a very early date.[3] Robert Ellrodt has made this distinction acutely and learnedly;[4] but it often seems unnecessarily sophisticated from a literary-critical point of view. I shall be content to try to show that there is rather more Neoplatonism in *The Faerie Queen* than

Ellrodt supposed, and that both traditions affect poetic forms not ordinarily thought of as carrying philosophic meaning.

Apart from a very few familiar passages of overtly allegorized metaphysics – such as the description of the Garden of Adonis – Spenser's most obvious expression of his philosophical vision takes the form of representing aspects of the divine image by sexually coupled contraries. He repeatedly imagines the divine as a union combining opposites in love – a thought in the same tradition with Dionysius's use of the word *henosis* both for divine unity and for sexual intercourse.[5] Thus, to mythologize the generation of life Spenser not only has a Titan-Chrysogone couple but also a Cupid-Psyche couple and a *Venus genetrix* combining with Adonis. Similarly, at the Temple of Venus Dame Concord, who 'divinely grew' and whose 'works divine did show' (IV.x.34), combines the contraries Love and Hate, two half-brothers, in her porch, while within *Venus hermaphroditus* (the composite deity Aphrodite-Hermes) is worshipped as an idol wearing a veil to signify esoterically the divine mystery of combination of sexual opposites: 'both kinds in one, / Both male and female, both under one name.'[6] Again in Book v Isis presents a double form. And in the Mutability Cantos Natura herself, the creative Logos, reconciles order and mutability in a veiled mystery uniting solar splendour and leonine terror.[7] Each of these double images brings to imaginative focus a prominent mythological passage containing a symbol of divinity. But human characters also may enact a similar quasi-mythic pattern: Scudamour and Amoret, embracing at the 1590 conclusion of Book III, resemble on their own level 'the fair hermaphrodite.' Both *Pagan Mysteries in the Renaissance* and *Spenser's Images of Life* relate these double images infolding contrary qualities to the Neoplatonic doctrine of *coincidentia oppositorum*, as set out in Nicholas of Cusa's *De docta ignorantia* or in the works of the Florentine Neoplatonists. And we may add the powerful influence of Francesco Colonna, whose *Hypnerotomachia* explores a sexual mysticism close to Spenser's formally, however different in tone and content.

Earlier, in his review of Ellrodt in *Études anglaises*,[8] Lewis noticed a peculiarity of some of Spenser's divine couples: namely, that the female partner dominates the male. It is Venus who possesses Adonis, not Adonis Venus. And she does so whenever she pleases: 'she her self, when ever that she will, / Possesseth him, and of his sweetness takes her fill' (iii.vi.46). As for Isis, she actually subdues Osyris in crocodile form beneath her foot and beats him with a rod.[9] A stern demonstration indeed that 'mercy is above this sceptred sway.'[10] But this odd female dominance becomes more intelligible, paradoxically, when we recall that in the Neoplatonic *coincidentia* neither opposite is subordinate to the other. The One transcends the many: it resolves differences not by favouring single elements of dualities, but by infolding both. How was Spenser to mythologize this doctrine? He could hardly have hit on a better symbol for the independence of contraries than feminine ascendancy. We have only to apply a transformational method, and restore ordinary (sixteenth-century) roles of masculine supremacy, to see how far the equality of Spenser's opposites depends on transposition of gender. Isis, for example, images 'that part of Justice, which is Equity' (v.vii.3), whereas Osyris is simple justice, a 'God of sovereign grace' (v.vii.2). Now if they had enjoyed a normal relation, Isis would inevitably have been relegated to subordinate status. But Spenser's conception of political order called for a quite different relation, one of scrupulous balance between equity (human rights, mercy, clemency) and justice (enforcement of sovereign power, 'stern behests,' 'cruel dooms'). A rough modern equivalent might be the need to weigh 'social justice' against 'law and order.' In an age of absolute monarchy Spenser needed to make an extreme counter-statement: Isis had to hold actual sway over Osyris for equity and justice both to be satisfied and at one. Only from such an interplay of fully realized conflicting values, from the opposition of contraries reconciled in the union Isis-Osyris, might the apocalyptic kingdom of peace, imaged by their issue Horus, emerge.[11]

A similar consideration may apply to other mythological works of Neoplatonic tendency, in which divine couples infold contrary values. One thinks of Botticelli's *Venus and Mars*, and of many representations of the god of strife disarmed or even bound by his peaceful opposite.

If divine couples are frequent and noticeable in *The Faerie Queen*, triads are still more frequent, noticeable, and striking. They appear both explicitly and implicitly, both as characters and as structural principles. Thus trios of characters, often siblings, are ubiquitous: Charissa-Fidelia-Speranza, Sansfoy-Sansloy-Sansjoy, Elissa-Medina-Perissa, Priamond-Diamond-Triamond, and Despetto-Decetto-Defetto, not to speak of the Fates, the Graces, Alma's counsellors, and such unnamed trios as the sons of Dolon or the foresters of iii.v. Discussing the triad at iv.ii.41–3, Wind, our best sybil through the caliginous shades of Renaissance Neoplatonism, detects that 'absence of discretion' in which 'a perfunctory handling of the Orphic rules could change a poet into a pedant' performing a mere 'didactic exercise' in the mystical unfolding of the triad. The verses, though fatuous, are so correct as to be useful as a model of 'explication' in the Neoplatonic sense. And you can see the force of this view: (iv.ii.42)

> Stout Priamond, but not so strong to strike,
> Strong Diamond, but not so stout a knight,
> But Triamond was stout and strong alike:
> On horseback used Triamond to fight,
> And Priamond on foot had more delight,
> But horse and foot knew Diamond to wield:
> With curtaxe used Diamond to smite,
> And Triamond to handle spear and shield,
> But spear and curtaxe both used Priamond in field.

I shall not defend the passage, though I suspect that it may once have seemed less fatuous, in context, than Wind implies. But notice the charge, of didactic and doctrinaire Neoplatonism. It is hardly one that readers of Ellrodt, or of current Spenser criticism, will be prepared for. Yet Wind's charge carries conviction: the passage closely resembles, not only in logical form but also in style, certain expansions of triads by philosophical authors. Ficino, in particular, distributes qualities symmetrically between terms with the same persistent speculative determination to permute triad after triad:

The devout soul directing itself towards God goes forward fortified by a certain three divine gifts or graces: sure faith, constant hope and ardent love (*caritas*). And it seems to offer its chief certainty of faith to the Son, its ardour of love to the Spirit, but its constancy of hope especially to the Father. So God joins the soul through attendant graces, again three in number: a new light, an incomparable joy, an invincible force. Thus the Son in particular seems to bestow light, and the Spirit joy, but the Father strength. Light is principally apportioned to faith, joy to hope and strength to love. These three are most certain arguments of the presence of God ... For this reason it is truly said 'The uneven number is pleasing to God' – that is, the triad, both in receiving and in giving.[12]

Spenser's triads are not generally, however, so crudely explicit. And those he develops on a structural scale have certainly at least been subtle enough to escape modern notice. Think of the elusive way, for example, in which the three sons of Aveugle function simultaneously as *exemplum* characters of middle scale and as indicators of large-scale structural triads. Perhaps on the principle of the whole in the part, all three, Sansjoy, Sansloy, and Sansfoy, appear in Book I – serving it seems as evil counterparts to the three theological virtues Charissa, Speranza, and Fidelia.[13] But Sansfoy is the only paynim brother finally disposed of in this book, presumably because its subject is precisely the defeat of infidelity. This defeat, not accomplished spiritually until the fight against the dragon, begins with the death of Sansfoy at 1.ii.19, which leads Redcrosse, through the victor's meed Duessa, to all the problems of distinguishing true and false religion. Sansloy reappears in Book II, surprisingly within quite a different scheme, as lover of Perissa (excessive pleasure) and opponent of the joyless puritanical Huddibras in the three-cornered fight at Medina's castle. Guyon has to avoid all excesses; still, his principal mission proves to be against Sansloy's extreme, 'lawless lust' as the Argument to 1.vi has it. Thus Book II indirectly brings Sansloy's end, as Book I finishes off Sansfoy. As for Sansjoy, he makes no personal appearance after 1.v.44, where he is left to recuperate in the care of Aesculapius. But the logic of the triad requires that Book III ought to achieve a decisive defeat, if not of Sansjoy, at least of what Sansjoy represents. And so it turns out, for the book largely consists of good and evil forms of joy. Malecasta's Castle Joyous offers false superficial joy: Malbecco keeps Hellenore 'Deprived of kindly joy and natural delight' (III.ix.5): and everywhere jealousy 'turnest love divine / To joyless dread' (III.xi.1). The culminating place of evil is Busyrane's, in which the 'joyance' of courtship becomes the joyless house of unhappy marriage; while the beneficent mythological centre is the Garden, where Adonis 'lives in everlasting joy' 'Joying his goddess, and of her enjoyed' (III.vi.48f.).

The progression *foi-loi-joi*, which no correspondence to the theological virtues can quite explain, I have elsewhere related to the familiar Neoplatonic triad *Veritas-Virtus-Amor* or *Fides-Honos-Amor*.[14] Valeriano expressed the first term of this so-called Triad of Fidius as *Veritas promissorum*, and it defines the subject of *Faerie Queen* I more adequately than might be supposed. For all Una's adventures demonstrate the power of divine truth and its relation to various forms of natural belief, superstition, error, and hypocrisy; while Redcrosse's troubles all begin with his failure to keep faith with Una. Redcrosse the 'Right faithful true' (I.i.2) is as much the patron of truth as of holiness; spiritual, moral, and intellectual truth being then so closely identified that Alciati could define faith as *constantia et veritas*. Similarly the second term of the Triad of Fidius, *Honos* or *Virtus*, corresponds closely to the subject of Book II. Belphoebe presents an icon of the far from irrelevant ideal *Honos*, as Philotime of its perverse form. And Guyon himself, guided by the divine truth of the Palmer, symbolizes Honour or Virtue in process of 'framing' or formation. Significantly, after he has fallen into disdainful self-righteous virtuousness at Mammon's Cave, it is an angelic divine *Amor* who reunites him with the Palmer's *Veritas*.[15] As for the third term *Amor*, its correspondence to the subject of *Faerie Queen* III is obvious enough: most would now agree that the book treats positive ideals of love, rather than chastity in any negative sense.

Less obviously Spenser exploits the structural possibilities of more fundamental triads adumbrated by that of Fidius and denoting parts of human nature itself: Pico's *Intellectus-Voluntas-Passio* and Ficino's *Mens-Ratio-Anima secunda*. The function of the intellectual part *mens* is to contemplate truth,[16] as Redcrosse does when he ascends the visionary mount of 1.x.53–68. Ideally the preoccupation of *mens* is single, in contrast to the multiplicity of the distractions of Error's serpent opinions.[17] But *mens* also communicates general truths to the faculty of moral choice (*ratio: voluntas: anima prima*). *Ratio* in turn reflects *mens*; translates its generalizations into action; and imposes its forms on the emotions. Hence the mirror relation of Books I and II; Guyon's obedience to the Palmer's precepts; and his opposition to passion of every sort (falsely formed emotion). Temperance receives a very broad interpretation in Book II because *ratio*'s functions extend throughout the moral sphere: Spenser's emphasis on the mean not only renders Aristotelian ethics but also Neoplatonic conceptions of *ratio* as a preserver of right proportion between mind and body.[18] More Neoplatonically still, the heroine of Book III embodies a love so much exalted above reason that she begins by overthrowing the knight of Temperance (III.i.6). Thus Britomart's counsellor, wise Glauce, though at first she tries to control the stirrings of tender passion, has to concede that 'love can higher stye [ascend], / Than reason's reach.'[19] Nevertheless this and all the loves of the third book remain rooted in *anima secunda*: even those of the Garden of Adonis, however much in contrast with Acrasia's, involve the same concupiscible faculty.

Anyone familiar with Neoplatonic thought will probably notice other structural triads, microcosmic and macrocosmic, in the three books of Part 1: perhaps the cosmic principles Light, Time, and Generation,[20] perhaps the triple stages of the soul's initiation, Dionysius's and Pico's *illuminari-purgari-perfici* triad.[21] The concern of Book I with mystery and revelation, with spiritual illumination and its obstacles, leads to an incidence of imagery of light and dark that strikes every careful reader. And the preoccupation of Book II with *purgari* is hardly less ineluctable. Ruddymane, Pyrochles, Tantalus, Pilate, and Maleger: all undergo symbolic immersion. Guyon's mission symbolizes mortification of the flesh and sanctification of the baptized body, while his descent into the Cave of Mammon can be construed as a purgative ordeal.[22] The correspondence of Book III to *perfici* is more abstract. It is explained by the book's presentation of pleasure, not only in person at III.vi.50, but implicitly throughout as the issue of love's interaction with the psyche. For the Neoplatonic *summum bonum* is pleasure, 'the supreme unmixed *voluptas*, which transcends the intellect altogether.'[23] Book III introduces for the first time a metaphysical background of ideal forms, the *rationes seminales* generated by Venus and Adonis, the parents of forms. We also notice Britomart's specially complete virtue and independence from Arthur's intervention.

Now obviously there is a danger, with a philosophy so flexible as Neoplatonism, of the critic imposing metaphysical patterns 'creatively.'[24] Nor can we yet decide whether Spenser's superimposition of triadic schemes springs from an ingenious mannerism of style or a more baroque and visionary syncretism thrusting towards an articulated trinitarian world view. But at least we may conclude that the 1590 publication of an instalment of three books indicates an organic structural division set off by close internal unity.

In the 1596 Part 2, Books IV–VI, other schemes emerge into prominence, notably the important triad *Animus-Corpus-Fortuna*, identified by Ficino with the Graces.[25] Ficino characteristically distinguished three graces within *Animus*, on the Procline principle of the 'whole in the part.'[26] Similarly Spenser makes the *Animus* term of his triad explicit in the titular episode of Book IV, the allegory of Triamond's infolding of his brothers' souls, which itself contains a triadic progression, as we have seen. And the theme of exchange of souls runs through all the book's friendships. Book V corresponds to *Corpus* more metaphorically and generally, in that it treats the just ordering of the body politic. In Book VI the *Fortuna* term is expressed through such prominent episodes as the tale of the unfortunate but stoic Meliboe and the vision of the Graces' gifts. More broadly, every interplay of heredity and nurture, advantage and need, appears as a disposition of the gifts of fortune.[27]

Ficino further identified the Graces with a moral triad *Veritas-Concordia-Pulchritudo*,[28] which is prominent in Part 2 of *The Faerie Queen*. For the Legend of Friendship is largely one of moral, political, and cosmic concord, Dame Concord herself appearing at iv.x. Truth in the political sense, honest simplicity, is just as obviously a subject of Book v: Astraea left the earth because 'no truth she found,' Talus's flail 'threshed out falsehood, and did truth unfold,' Mercilla judged Duessa or Falsehood, and Artegall condemned Burbon because 'Knights ought be true.' As for Book vi, it not only introduces the Graces of Beauty themselves, but contrasts beauty of manners and beauty of outward shows in countless ways. The preoccupation is traceable even in characters' names: Mirabella, Calidore, Calepine.

Again, Part 2 also expands the fundamental triad *emanatio-raptio-remeatio*. We find *emanatio* in the offerings at the Temple of Venus and the generative efflux of rivers at the spousal of Thames and Medway (iv); *raptio* or *conversio* in Britomart's vision at Isis Church and in Artegall's magisterial reforms (v); *remeatio* in the courteous restitution of gifts 'in greater store' and in the repeated return of child to parent (vi).[29]

Even from this very brief schematic survey it will have been noticed that Part 2 triads also occur in Part 1 and *vice versa*. Thus we need only compare the House of Holiness and the Castle of Alma to see correspondences of Books i and ii with terms of the *Animus-Corpus-Fortuna* triad. And Book iii celebrates *Fortuna* by the new Ariostan fortuitousness of its narrative technique and by its elevation of the very *Tyche* or 'occasion' that makes ideal forms variable (iii.vi.38), and that in consequence appeared in Book ii as a dangerous or evil principle.[30] Here the terms follow the same order in each part. Other recurring triads, however, have their terms permuted, according to a Neoplatonic practice followed especially by Ficino.[31] Thus the Triad of Fidius reappears in Part 2 as *Amor-Veritas-Virtus*, and the moral interpretation of the Graces has been foreshadowed in a subordinate *Veritas-Concordia-Pulchritudo* triad in Part 1. (*Concordia* in Book ii is an inner psychological or moral concord of mental faculties: *Pulchritudo* in Book iii is the pursuit of Florimell.) Thus we arrive at the scheme

i	ii	iii	iv	v	vi
Veritas	Honos	Amor	Amor	Veritas	Honos
Veritas	Concordia	Pulchritudo	Concordia	Veritas	Pulchritudo

To some extent this may all be the outcome simply of a trinitarian habit of mind. (Even Ficino's triadic expansions often suggest a religious stance rather than a consistent system.) But the habit was in all probability largely conscious, and deliberately adopted to introduce an element of controlled tonal variety. Thus Books III and IV are both about love; but in one case *Amor* is modulated by *Pulchritudo*, in the other by *Concordia*. The successive overlapping permutations and combinations of themes avoid a crude abruptness that might have resulted from simple changes of subject from book to book.

It is reasonable to assume that the remaining fragment of *The Faerie Queen* represents only a few of the modulating progressions through which the permutations of its triads would have been carried in the complete work, and that in this respect it resembles those Neoplatonic works conceived in a cyclical spirit, whose historical disfiguration Wind has mourned. How the subjects of the remaining books would have been arranged, we can only speculate. But it seems not unlikely that Spenser planned two further groups of three subjects, each involving a cardinal virtue in the middle place, permuting the triads already examined and perhaps introducing others.

I turn to an example of middle scale, one of the most rigorous yet also poetically satisfying of the poem's Neoplatonic exercises: the dance of the Graces, mythic paradigm of all triads.[32] Spenser emphasizes the focal value of this image by the alienation effect, rare with him, of autobiographical treatment. For Colin's vision at the physical centre of twelve purposed books epitomizes his creator's confrontation of his imagined world.[33] Significantly, from the present standpoint, the cosmic pattern Colin beholds is a *choresis*, or metaphysical dance, unfolding in triple rhythm the entire beauty of Venus the formgiver: (VI.x.15)

> Those were the Graces, daughters of delight,
> Handmaids of Venus, which are wont to haunt
> Upon this hill, and dance there day and night:
> Those three to men all gifts of grace do grant,
> And all, that Venus in her self doth vaunt,
> Is borrowed of them.

Colin explains the Graces after they have vanished (a chastening sequence for interpreters to reflect upon), by moralizing them under three heads. These are: facial expression, nakedness, and posture. Under each aspect, characteristically, Spenser discovers triads of qualities, though these disclose themselves in a variety of ways: (VI.x.24)

1 Therefore they always smoothly seem to smile,
   That we likewise should mild and gentle be,
2 And also naked are, that without guile
   Or false dissemblance all them plain may see,
   Simple and true from covert malice free:
3 And eek them selves so in their dance they bore,
   That two of them still forward[34] seemed to be,
   But one still towards showed her self afore;
   That good should from us go, than come in greater store.

Wind's *Pagan Mysteries in the Renaissance* has set out the philosophical content of the Graces' iconography, and particularly of their 2 + 1 choreographic figure, with a fullness and subtlety it would be graceless to try to repeat.[35] But we may notice the poetic means whereby Spenser mimes their figure. First, take the grammatical structure. Each aspect seems to be given a description, then a moralisation introduced by *that* = 'in order that.' But two descriptions are in terms of seeming, one in terms of being: the Graces 'seem' to smile so that we should be similarly mild; they 'are' naked so that we may see them plainly; and two of them 'seemed' outward turned so that we may follow their example of generous action. Even the verbs join in the Graces' dance. Or consider the aspects in turn. The Graces smile 'smoothly' (one quality) to make us 'mild and gentle' (two qualities). Here three qualities are divided 2 + 1 between mankind and the Graces. Their nakedness, however, presents triads in a different way. Its purpose is that all may see them 'plain' (one positive) 'without guile or false dissemblance' (two negatives): 'simple and true' (two positives) 'from covert malice free' (one negative). That is, positives and negatives form the 2 + 1 configuration. Next, the Graces exemplify generosity precisely by the 2 + 1 dance figure: two seem facing 'forward' (i.e., outward), only one inward turned. Finally, taking all three aspects, we notice that while the first and third display single triads, the second offers a double triad. Again the 2 + 1 figure, whose cosmic meaning is generosity, liberality, ultimately the creative spirit of grace itself. And the outgoing movement may also be seen in the progression of the beholders' attitudes, from an inner response of gentle mildness, through a reciprocal phase of looking, to the outward response of giving.

But is this all? So far we have only treated the most obvious chain of discourse. But actually the stanza is full of syntactic, semantic, and schematic ambiguities. Are the Graces naked so that we can see that they are without guile, or so that we may see them without using guile? And what of the semantic ambiguity that allows us to take 'simple and true from covert malice free' as the third aspect? There would then be a progression from seeming (aspect 1) through exposure (aspect 2) to inner moral meaning. This movement, moreover, would be appropriately dia-stolic: the Graces seem smooth so that we may be gentle; they are outwardly naked (that is, without disguise) so that all may see them openly; and all for their part see the Graces as they inwardly are, simple and true. The third, covert aspect, mime-tically, has no introductory physical description, but comprises three simple moral qualities. On this analysis the explanation of the dance in lines 5–9 would be a summary, referring to all three aspects treated symmetrically, a triad of qualities being assigned to each. This ambiguity extends to minor details: 'seemed to be' (line 7) can be regarded as a recapitulatory infolding of seeming and being. In short, ingeniously varied schemes throughout cor-respond to the triad and its shifting divisions into proceeding and reverting phases. And this emphasis, as we know, characterised Renaissance Neoplatonism, not the earlier Neoplatonism of such authors as Dionysius.[36]

All through Book VI the triad of the Graces undergoes repeated expansion and travesty. Everyone has noticed, for example, that Despetto, Decetto, and Defetto constitute an evil antitype; though fewer, perhaps, have traced the correspondences of individual terms of the antitriad with aspects of the Graces. Timias' attackers are introduced in a stanza whose metaphysical inspiration will by now be readily appreciated: (VI.v.13)

The first of them by name was called Despetto,
Exceeding all the rest in power and height;
The second not so strong but wise, Decetto;
The third nor strong nor wise, but spitefullest Defetto.

The powerful loftiness of Despetto[37] exactly opposes the mild gentle smiling of the Graces. Similarly the Graces' *nuda sinceritas*, their plain guilelessness, contrasts with Decetto's[38] deceitfulness or 'false dissemblance'; and their simple truth with the ungenerous faultfinding ('covert malice') of Defetto.[39] The antitriad even receives an iconographical expression equivalent to that of the Graces in the attack on Timias. For proud Despetto is the only adversary who attacks frontally, while Decetto tries to 'circumvent' Timias, spiteful Defetto to destroy him behind his back.

The qualities of the Graces and anti-Graces alike find expansion in the several episodes of Book vi. Graham Hough's opinion, that 'it would be absurd to look for formal allegorical significance' (page 205) in the early episodes of the book, might itself be called absurd, were that not to risk Despetto. Consider Disdain, who walks on tiptoe on brittle legs, who stares with unsmiling 'stern eyebrows' (vi.viii.26), and who with Scorn abuses Mirabella in 'foul despite' (vi.viii.6): is he not an expansion of Despetto? And surely the same applies to Mirabella herself, at whose trial for cruelty in love 'fell Despite / Gave evidence' (vi.vii.34). The Disdain and Scorn she suffers punishment from are her own: they have become habitual, so that even when she takes pity on Timias scornful disdain is punishing to both. Crudor develops Despetto in a less psycho-pathological vein. The reverse of 'mild and gentle,' he roughly exacts a service in love for which he makes no return. As Kathleen Williams has remarked,[40] the 'movement of the circle' completed by the Graces is here reversed. In the same way tricky Turpine doubles the deceits of Decetto, contriving to 'cloak' his mischief, until Arthur strips him of his courteous disguise, despoils and 'baffles' him (vi.vii.4,26–7). Meanwhile the Blattant Beast nips in from time to time to show up Defetto.

Triad and antitriad also function structurally, with their terms alternating as in a dance, now within a canto, now at greater length. Canto vi, for example, unfolds all three terms: the hermit explains the Blattant Beast (Defetto); Mirabella in penance exhibits her Despetto; and Arthur deceives Turpine, whose wounded body is concealed by Blandina (Decetto). In the early cantos the development of sophisticated virtue takes forms easily missed or even mistaken for contraries to the Graces. Thus, faced with Despetto's oppression of helpless victims, the virtuous knights at first seem themselves 'despiteous' and crude. Calidore butchers Maleffort, Tristram the Knight of the Summer Barge; until we badly need a reminder that 'Blood is no blemish' (vi.i.26). Similarly Calidore is capable of conspiring in deceptions to circumvent the compromising position Priscilla's guileless simplicity has betrayed her into (iii.18), or to restore marital harmony between Matilda and Bruin (iv.34–8). And Arthur twice deceives Turpine, once quite deviously, by getting Enias to lie for him. Looking more closely, however, we see an aspect of the Graces developed in each episode. Calidore remains mild under the nagging reproaches of Briana. His white lies to Priscilla's father, like Arthur's various deceptions, are the 'sweet semblant' of the gracious courtier, which no courteous reader will long confuse with Decetto's malicious falsity. And the knights who are surprised unarmed making love – Aladine with Priscilla, Calepine with Serena[41] – manifest to the charitable eye a complementary quality of the Graces, guileless nakedness.

The last cantos penetrate to the Grace's meaning, liberality and the conception of Grace itself. They are filled with images of generosity: Calidore's kindness to the miserable Coridon, and his repeated readiness to give his life for Pastorella; Meliboe's hospitality to Calidore; and the outgoing love at great cost of Claribell and Bellamour. By contrast most of the evil characters are now thieves, not because the criminal classes are specially impolite, but because they lack the grace of giving. This is so, whether you consider the lustful savage thieves who grudge even to share Serena with their fellow cannibals, or the brigands – so contrary to generous Meliboe that they soon cause his death – who deal in human lives and freedom for the sake of their own security, or even, by slave-trading, for gain, and who kill their own captain as soon as he treats Pastorella personally enough to desire her love; down to the Blattant Beast itself, which, though it includes all those discourtesies classified under Defetto, is in these cantos known by its spoil (xii.22) and its thefts from the clergy (xii.23,25). Calidore's own part in Book vi has a triadic rhythm of one proceeding and two reverting phases. For, after a first period of virtuous (reverting) activity, during his so-called truancy he mainly receives benefits, such as Meliboe's hospitality, and seems to forget his mission. Finally, inspired by his glimpse of the Graces (a poetic vision proceeding from the divine), he enters on another reverting phase of activity. His truancy, then, may not be a moral failure quite like those of the other knights patron, but rather a life-stage. Kathleen Williams[42] thinks that he temporarily forgets his responsibility to make return for life's benefits, which in a sense is true. But one almost feels that the 'fault' serves partly as a means of provoking blame and hence an encounter with the Blattant Beast of defamation. After all Calidore could hardly have defeated the Beast if his own culpability had been very great. There is a remarkable alienation effect here, whereby Spenser, in what from some points of view is his most serious book, comes near to questioning with Meliboe the whole validity of the court as an image of glory.

These structural extensions and replications of the triad in multiplicities of dazzlingly intricate forms are constructs of art, not exercises in philosophy. Still Spenser may have found a suggestion for an aim for his artistic endeavours in the Neoplatonic conception, developed by Pico, Ficino, and others, that every part of the universe is a triadic microcosm of the whole, in which the contemplative observer may see vestiges of the Trinity through its very texture: *Divinam trinitatem in rebus cunctis agnosces.*[43] Alternatively, he may have been influenced by the mediaeval tradition, going back to SS Augustine and Bonaventura, that traced a trinitarian pattern in operations of the human mind.[44]

More generally, Platonism informs the relation of personal image to idea throughout *The Faerie Queen*. All the main characters are 'images of virtues, vices,' and so imply a system of ideas and images of ideas. By the same Platonic compliment that Drayton paid in *Idea's Mirror* and Sidney in *Astrophil and Stella* xxv,

Spenser elevates Queen Elizabeth to the realm of ideas. Consequently he may 'express' her in more than one image – in Una, Medina,[45] Britomart, and Mercilla, as well as in Belphoebe and Gloriana.[46] On the other hand, he usually needs several of the Queen's subjects to make up the particular intention of a single image. Both Leicester and Essex resemble Artegall, as the contemporary Cambridge Marginalian noted.[47] We recall Xenophon's account of the process of idealization by which the artist combines features from many individuals in constructing one ideal figure.[48]

The status of images in *The Faerie Queen* has been treated generally by Lewis in *Spenser's Images of Life*. Here I shall only take up the point that in the lower register of the cosmic scale – farthest from reality – the relation between image and idea is that of false to true. The shibboleth 'appearance and reality,' currently a fashionable theme to carve out of almost any Elizabethan work, has here some meaning still. As in the Platonic system, so in *The Faerie Queen*, imitations are less good than originals (though not necessarily evil), so that the reader aspires to ideas of divine beauty and virtue by rejecting, or else by loving and transcending, 'mere' images.

Sometimes this distinction receives narrative enactment. Thus Spenser more than once portrays an evil perversion of good as the fabrication of a double. Archimago tempts Redcrosse away from Una by abusing his fantasy 'with false shows' of her disloyalty. He (i.i.45–6)

> Had made a lady of that other sprite,
> And framed of liquid air her tender parts
> So lively, and so like in all men's sight,
> That weaker sense it could have ravished quite ...

> And that new creature born without her due,
> Full of the maker's guile, with usage sly
> He taught to imitate that lady true,
> Whose semblance she did carry under feigned hue.

Later in the same book Redcrosse himself is impersonated to deceive Una, and in Book III Florimell is copied by a witch who constructs Snowy Florimell, a false image that some to their cost prefer. But the most elaborate impersonation is Busyrane's magic conjuring of idols of Cupid. His cruel Cupid easily deceives, for Cupid in the world is always cruel. Thus the Cupid on Scudamour's shield has 'cruel shafts'; that of the Garden has returned from ransacking the world with spoils and cruelty (III.vi.49). But the true Cupid is cruel not of himself, but only through the world's accidents; whereas Busyrane raises false images, 'a thousand monstrous forms,' of a passion that ends in cruelty absolute and unthinkable. Spenser's insistence on the false imagery is psychologically acute. Busyrane has filled his house with tapestries and reliefs showing the tyrannous cruelty of Cupid in triumph; not to mention a statue of Cupid maiming the guardian of chastity – in short, a whole culture of erotic images, which Britomart must contemplate, live with, and be conditioned by, before he can subject her imagination, by his charms, to the masque of Cupid. This at first seems a nuptial performance by the god himself; but it too proves illusory when Britomart passes beyond images of fantasy, through the iron gate of life, to the inner and comparatively real image of sex.

Even where Spenser introduces no outright *Doppelgänger* or false image, a similar opposition of evil imitation to good reality may be implicit. Throughout, moral emblems, mythological entities, and symbolic attributes often appear twice over, in true and in false forms, which can scarcely be understood separately from one another. For a characteristic *modus operandi* of Spenser's imagination leads to pairs of iconographically similar passages in close moral relation, even at wide spatial remove.[49] This may be why *The Faerie Queen* seems morally obscure to some, who perhaps read it too seldom to make those connections between disjunct passages on which its meaning depends. And the same applies to criticisms of disunity and structural weakness levelled not only at Spenser, but also at such later authors using a constructive method learned from him, as Fielding and Defoe.

Everyone has noticed the correspondence and contrast that Spenser develops between the Bower of Bliss and the Garden of Adonis. Each place is a Garden of Life, in each a genius keeps the gate – in the Garden of Adonis the true Agdistes, (II.xii.47)

> that celestial power, to whom the care
> Of life, and generation of all
> That lives, pertains in charge particular,
> Who wondrous things concerning our welfare,
> And strange phantoms doth let us oft foresee,
> And oft of secret ill bids us beware:
> That is our self ...

but in the Bower a being (II.xii.48)

> quite contrary,
> The foe of life, that good envies to all,
> That secretly doth us procure to fall,
> Through guileful semblants, which he makes us see.

Over one a lustful *Venus naturalis* presides, over the other a creative *Venus genetrix*. The good Venus enjoys an Adonis who has lived through death, transformation, and rebirth to everlasting joy; the evil Venus, Acrasia, enjoys a Verdant who sleeps forever in life's selfish springtime. Finally, both places have a symbol of chaos, or chaotic sensuality: Grill, declining to be restored from hoglike to higher form; and the boar, safely imprisoned under the Garden Mount by Venus the formgiver.[50]

No one could miss these echoes, which sound loudly even in the ears of Momus. But we must read often to hear the overtones of a more delicate order. Thus, the Bower of Bliss fountain is built of a mysterious unnamed substance: (II.xii.60)

> a fountain stood,
> Of richest substance, that on earth might be,
> So pure and shiny, that the silver flood
> Through every channel running one might see;
> Most goodly it with curious imagery
> Was overwrought,

and with shapes of wanton *putti*. Now Spenser reintroduces the same transparent material at the Temple of Venus, where Scudamour releases Amoret from maidenhood. But this time it takes the religious form of an altar, or, by Empsonian ambiguity, of an *idol* of Venus: (IV.x.39–40)

Right in the midst the goddess' self did stand
Upon an altar of some costly mass,
Whose substance was uneath to understand:
For neither precious stone, nor dureful brass,
Nor shining gold, nor mouldering clay it was;
But much more rare and precious to esteem,
Pure in aspect, and like to crystal glass,
Yet glass was not, if one did rightly deem,
But being fair and brickle, likest glass did seem.

But it in shape and beauty did excel
All other idols ...

I believe we are to connect these passages and infer that the
Bower dissipates libido from the sexual vessel in a formless
stream (the fountain of will), whereas the Temple offers it in
personal form. True, Acrasia's fountain seems outwardly semi-
personal, its exterior being 'overwrought'[51] with 'curious
imagery' of *putti*. But in the better instance the mysterious sub-
stance shapes an altar with an identified image of Venus, said to
be superior to any the pagan world had to offer. In other words
the Temple exists for Christian sacrifice of love, not merely for
expression of will. Taken separately, neither mention of material
is very significant; brought together, they are full of meaning.
Not only do they persuade that self-expression is less personal
than love that oblates personal identity; but they also connect
the transparent flesh of the fountain with the brittle glass-like
substance of marital loyalty,[52] already introduced in iii.ii.

Generalizing further, we may almost formulate a natural law
of Spenser's Fairyland: At least one corresponding evil image
precedes a virtuous image. The house of proud Lucifera, where
the non-porter Malvenù denies no one, precedes the house of
Holiness, where Humilitá warily guards a 'straight and narrow'
way. Similarly the bad Venus of the Bower comes earlier than
any good Venus, the bad Adonis of Malecasta's tapestry earlier
than the Adonis of the Garden, and many cruel or ambivalent
Cupids before the 'mild' Cupid of vi.vii.37, Mirabella's judge: a
tetrad of false friends, Ate-Duessa-Blandamour-Paridell, traves-
ties in advance the true tetrad of concord, Triamond-Cambell-

Canacee-Cambina: and authority seems evil in the proud, testy, status-conscious Artegall of iv.iv–vi, before it is shown virtuous in the reformed co-ruling Artegall of Britomart's dream of state at Isis Church and in the regal Mercilla. It is the same with the two tournaments. The discordant cestus tournament of Book iv degenerates into disorderly strife, with Artegall going off in 'great displeasure'[53] and even Britomart leaving when 'she them saw to discord set' (iv.v.29); the tournament of v.iii, however, after the achievement of concord, is characterized by felicitous order, only temporarily disturbed by Braggadocchio's false claim.

Sometimes the approach to an image of virtue goes more ceremoniously through several graduated stages, first of evil, then of neutral or natural images. Thus Spenser leads up to the visionary ring of maidens about the Graces' ring, through descriptions of the concentric circles of friendly or amorous shepherdesses and swains garlanding Pastorella (herself crowned with flowers), from the cluster of greedy robbers surrounding Serena, who lust after her and only grudgingly give her up to their evil god, in dark imitation of the return of graces to the all-giver.

One cannot adequately discuss such correspondences in terms of moral contrast. For that, Spenser had no need to design so elaborate a system of paired images. Where the images are mythological, one can relate them to the astrological and Neoplatonic doctrine that the same deity may exert either an excessive (bad) or a harmoniously modified (good) influence.[54] In general, however, it seems reasonable to construe them as simply Platonic. The movement from false images to true belongs to a larger movement from the world of appearances towards that of reality and ideas.

So regarded, the poem as a whole may be described as an allegorical expansion of Arthur's quest for Gloriana through reflections of her glory on individual ideals or images of virtues. In abstract terms, this is the quest of eros for the heavenly beauty, and as such it can find no fulfilment in any good short of the highest of all, good itself. By apparent goods it is betrayed. Hence only a vagrant 'fancy' and a 'semblant vain' makes Arthur wish that the Florimell he follows (III.iv.54)

> mote be
> His Faerie Queen, for whom he did complain:
> Or that his Faerie Queen were such, as she ...

Nevertheless his error hardly seems ignoble: Florimell's short-coming is simply that of necessity she can only image the one true fair. Thus Arthur's pursuit corresponds on a loftier plane to pursuit of false Florimell by baser characters: as the false Flori-mell is to the true, so is the true to Gloriana.[55] From this pro-portional relation large inferences can be drawn. For example, adopting Angus Fletcher's terminology we may say that the heroes of *The Faerie Queen*, especially the titular knights patron, function as subcharacters generated by Arthur.[56] A passage in Toscanella, cited by William Nelson in another connection, is very relevant here. Ariosto's commentator says that his author 'placed several virtues in several individuals, one virtue in one character and another in another character, in order to fashion out of all the characters a well-rounded and perfect man. A well-rounded and perfect man is one adorned with all the virtues.'[57] In Spenser's view the 'well-rounded and perfect man' displays mag-nificence; 'which virtue,' the Letter to Ralegh tells us, 'is the per-fection of all the rest, and containeth in it them all.' And not only does Arthur's magnificence contain the individual virtues, but in each book in turn it issues in 'deeds ... appliable to that virtue.' Consequently the Legend of Temperance finds Arthur temperate and struggling with Maleger, arch-enemy of the temperate body; the Legend of Friendship finds him intervening between com-batants, 'With gentle words persuading them to friendly peace' (IV.ix.32).

This helps to answer some common criticisms of Spenser's overall narrative structure.[58] We defend the unity of a single book by saying, in effect, that its significant content is allegorical, out-wardly symbolized by actions of subcharacters but inwardly attributable to the knight patron. And in the same way we may defend the linking narrative, by saying that Arthur approaches his goal allegorically through the symbolic actions of his sub-characters, the champions of virtues. Like the heroes of individual books, Arthur is morally imperfect. Like them, too, he is not even invariably superior to his subcharacters: Scudamour and Brito-mart have to restrain him from killing Paridell and his cronies, just as Amoret earlier taught Britomart to spare Busyrane. More dubiously, Mirabella persuades him not to kill Disdain, almost as Mammon persuaded Guyon not to contend with this fault at all.[59]

Here Fletcher's theory of the generation of subcharacters requires modification. If one thinks of the allegorical hero as generating other characters, who serve to objectify traits of his personality, one must also think of him as generating a fictive self. For he himself participates in the fiction with the subcharac-ters. He speaks, struggles, and has dealings with them: he inhabits their world. It is much the same with certain dreams. You generate in them not only symbolic people but also, very often, a dreamer who represents yourself. Represents you, but cannot be wholly identified with you – since you, after all, are having the dream. The relation of dreamer or hero to subcharacters becomes almost explicit in *The Faerie Queen* when Arthur dreams a vision of Gloriana.[60] For Arthur's visitant, who talked throughout the night ('Ne living man like words did ever hear, / As she to me delivered all that night') is a character in his dream. But he is a character in it too. On waking he finds 'pressed grass, where she had lyen.' And from that moment his waking experience extends his dream, as he pursues in life the ego-ideal he dreamt. To change the figure, he goes on to enact the epic Gloriana recited to him in his vision. Significantly this all begins at a time when he is given over to the pleasures of 'looser life.'

Arthur's quest takes him towards Gloriana in a movement that for him must mysteriously take the time of all twelve yearly adventures, though the other heroes seem to attend the court at least annually. Moreover, all the other quests start at court, in-stead of being directed towards it. This pattern is hardly intel-ligible, except from a Neoplatonic point of view. In terms of the doctrine of the triad, however, it makes good sense. For in Ar-thur's quest through individual virtues we see a large-scale *choresis* or triadic movement. The source of the virtues manifested *seriatim* is Gloriana in her divine general intention, so that Arthur's search for her is the returning phase (*remeatio*) of the cosmic rhythm. Spenser himself puts it like this, in the Proem to Book VI, where he addresses Queen Elizabeth the 'special intention' of Gloriana:

> Then pardon me, most dreaded sovereign,
> That from your self I do this virtue bring,
> And to your self do it return again:
> So from the ocean all rivers spring,
> And tribute back repay as to their king.
> Right so from you all goodly virtues well
> Into the rest, which round about you ring,
> Fair lords and ladies, which about you dwell,
> And do adorn your court, where courtesies excel.

This stanza hints broadly enough why the questing knights issue from Gloriana's court to perform their virtuous deeds. With the help of a suggestion of Maurice Evans's[61] it is not difficult to work out that the missions correspond to the Neoplatonic *emanatio*, the quests themselves to the *raptio* or *conversio*, and the ingathering of the virtues in the complete person of Arthur to the return or *remeatio*. Or, to construe the sequence personally, an inner spiritual prompting (the dream of glory that is the divine offering or *emanatio*) initiates a life-long *askesis*, or mystical way, through virtues to the inclusive integration of the whole man or divine image. Spenser combines the allegorical mode with a well suited philosophical model, in eloquent expression of the experience of vocation.

Some who accept the idea of an overall movement throughout the poem will look for development of character, and be disappointed, even with respect to the allegory symbolized by the generated narratives. This disappointment is unreasonable: Spenser never intended *The Faerie Queen* as a *Bildungsroman*. But it is also unreasonable to rush with Nelson (page 122) to the opposite extreme pedagogically, of expecting the characters to be completely static, or 'stable.' We are bound to look at least for moral progression in Arthur and the knights patron. To take the more difficult case, Arthur's, a progression can legitimately be found in his manifesting virtues in a logical and organic sequence.

Each of his virtues transcends its predecessor. When Britomart meets Guyon she overthrows him through the 'secret virtue' (III.i.10) of her enchanted spear, because chaste love is a higher virtue than temperance, presupposing it as a *sine qua non*. Similarly the third knight is able to rescue the first, in the unequal fight before the House of Malecasta. And Guyon in his quest seeks to arrest concupiscence – a mission one might define theologically as mortification of the flesh and destruction of the body of sin, or as sanctification; the next stage after the baptism of repentance Book I was concerned with. Try a transformation, putting Book II before Book I, and you arrive at an unacceptably Arminian theological argument, not to speak of an incoherent psychological sequence. Moving to Part 2, we find similar evidences of progression: justice in Book v takes for granted the concord, alliances, and social contract established in Book IV; but its rough hero Artegall must suffer the Blattant Beast quelled in Book VI.[62] In short, Arthur's moral or erotic aspiration is not a story manifesting virtues in random order, nor exhibiting facets of a static character; but rather imitating a search for moral glory and complete integration, through the insufficiencies of individual virtues, each of which transcends and includes its predecessor. The well-rounded man turns out to be a little like the concentric moral spheres on the title page of John Case's *De sphaera civitatis*, where the outermost *primum mobile* reaches to the queen herself and therefore contains all virtues.

From the point of view of consistency of structure *The Faerie Queen* is really extraordinarily unified, however strange a description of it that has come to seem. The dispute about unity has been partly semantic: some mean unity in Ariosto's or Milton's or Sterne's or Proust's sense; others the unity of Minturno, Waldock, Addison, and Hough.

If *The Faerie Queen* bodies forth a consistent philosophical vision, the questions next arise whether it is a philosophical poem, and what relation the philosophy bears to the poetry. It seems at least as philosophical as, say, Wordsworth's *Prelude*; though not often philosophical in a systematic sense. I have emphasized structural patterning; but every reader knows that *The Faerie Queen* is free from any unnatural rage for order. It never discloses its form to us, except in piecemeal fashion, pattern by pattern by apparent pattern; gradually, as if you were learning the laws of a real world. Spenser is seldom doctrinaire like Dante, or Blake, or (in a different way) e. e. cummings. Nevertheless, his philosophy not only serves a useful purpose: it also seems true.

Aesthetically considered, a Neoplatonic model was good for *The Faerie Queen*. It gave intellectual structure, while allowing room for delicate shades of individual feeling. Spenser's philosophy of moral aspiration, his love-relation with the one true fair, has an elusive unifying function not unlike that of the search for personal identity in Proust; though of course very different substantively. Since his philosophy was not the poet's own construction, it never distracted him from his true calling, exploration of the inner universe of sensibility. That exploration he carried out with an unusual integration of feeling, which gives the poem coherence even when it is not overtly concerned with unity or reconciliation of opposites. Yet the latter bulks so large that we must count it a great loss not to have the parts of *The Faerie Queen* in which its larger contraries would have been brought to narrative resolution.

But the aesthetic advantages of Spenser's philosophy are far from being only negative or neutral. The flexible metaphysics of Neoplatonism suited his temperament and art as Scholasticism would never have done: we need only compare the firm, even rigid, division of the *Divina Commedia* with the fluid metamorphic movement of *The Faerie Queen* to see that. This is not meant primarily as a value judgment. However, the two philosophies have come to differ in status so oddly that their relative value invites attention. And Spenser's poem is important evidence of Neoplatonism's fertile and beneficent influence on the arts. In that respect *The Faerie Queen* ranks with the finest works produced by the Medici circle. To go on from this claim to say that Neoplatonic forms are only a subset of the range of structures composing this encyclopedic yet Christian epic, is to give some idea, perhaps, of its stature.

1 'Spenser's *Faerie Queene*,' in *The Age of Chaucer*, ed. Boris Ford (Harmondsworth, 1954), p. 219: 'Given the definite, though disguised dependence of the whole allegorical scheme upon medieval habits of thought, the result is a structure that has ceased to hold together, a dislocation of what might have been, as in Langland it still was, a varied and coherent unity'; cf. p. 223, '*The Faerie Queene* ... in great part belies its own claims to architectural structure.' For a criticism of the assumptions underlying comparisons of *The Faerie Queen* to a disordered Gothic cathedral, drawn by John Hughes (1715) and Richard Hurd (1762), see René Wellek and Austin Warren, *Theory of Literature* (New York, 1956), p. 131.

2 See J. Shearman, *Mannerism* (Harmondsworth, 1967), e.g., p. 125; also Franzsepp Würtenberger, *Mannerism*, tr. Michael Heron (New York, Chicago, and San Francisco, 1963).

3 Strictly speaking, the single orthodox Neoplatonic system, to which many Renaissance scholars have found it convenient to refer, has never had a real existence: differences, even between the systems of Pico and Ficino, obstinately divide the parts of the chimera.

4 *Neoplatonism in the Poetry of Spenser*, Travaux d'Humanisme et Renaissance xxxv (Geneva, 1960).

5 C.E. Rolt, *Dionysius the Areopagite on the Divine Names and the Mystical Theology* (New York, 1957), p. 60, n. 5; cf. Philo, *De opificio mundi*, tr. F.H. Colson and G.H. Whitaker (Cambridge, Mass. and London, 1939), I, 13–14.

6 IV.x.41: 'The cause why she was covered with a veil, / Was hard to know, for that her priests the same / From people's knowledge laboured to conceal. / But sooth it was not sure for womanish shame, / Nor any blemish, which the work mote blame; / But for, they say, she hath both kinds in one, / Both male and female, both under one name: / She sire and mother is her self alone, / Begets and eke conceives, ne needeth other none.' See C.S. Lewis, *Spenser's Images of Life* (Cambridge, 1967), pp. 41–4; Edgar Wind, *Pagan Mysteries in the Renaissance* (London, 1958), pp. 172ff. Throughout this paper the spelling of quotations from Spenser is modernized (except for proper names), but the original punctuation of 1596 retained. For a rationale of this type of editorial procedure see *The Poems of John Milton*, ed. John Carey and Alastair Fowler (London, 1968), pp. x–xi.

7 For the Neoplatonic background of this image see Lewis, p. 15.

8 *Études anglaises* 14 (1961), 111f.

9 v.vii.7,15. A priest of Isis Church reveals the identity of the crocodile at v.vii.22.

10 *Merchant of Venice* IV.i.189.

11 Horus is represented by the 'lion of great might' of v.vii.16.

12 Marsilio Ficino, *Opera omnia*, 2 vols. (Basel, 1576), i, 443: '*Pius quidem animus ad Deum se convertens, tribus quibusdam gratiis divinitus munitus incedit, fide certa, spe firma, charitate ferventi. Certitudinem quidem fidei filio potissimum offerre videtur, amoris ardorem spiritui,*

*spei firmitatem praecipue patri. Deus igitur tribus quoque gratiis comi-
tantibus convenit in animum, novo quodam lumine, incomparabili
gaudio, invicto vigore. Lumen quidem filius praecipue videtur afferre.
Gaudium autem spiritus, Pater vero vigorem. Lumen fidei praecipue
distribuitur, spei gaudium, amori denique vigor. Tria haec ipsius
praesentia Dei certissima sunt argumenta ... Quapropter iure dictum:
Numero Deus impare gaudet, id est, ternario, tum in recipiendo, tum
in dando.'*

13 This correspondence is proposed by William Nelson in *The Poetry of
Edmund Spenser* (New York and London, 1963), pp. 154–5; we need
not accept his fanciful suggestion of a further correspondence with
Hooker's quite untriadic series of qualities: 'infidelity, extreme despair,
hatred of God and all godliness, obduration in sin.'

14 *Spenser and the Numbers of Time* (London, 1964), pp. 22, 143; see
P.L. Williams, 'Two Roman Reliefs in Renaissance Disguise,' *Journal
of the Warburg Institute* 4 (1941), where the origins of the Triad of
Fidius are discussed. Casual use by Ficino (I, 845, l. 1) suggests that the
scheme was familiar in Neoplatonic circles.

15 On the need for *Amor* to unite *Fides* and *Honos*, see Alciati's account
of the Triad of Fidius in *Emblemata*, ed. Claude Minois (Paris, 1608),
p. 86.

16 Ficino, I, 269–70; cf. 90: '*Mens enim tua veritatem quaerit*'; and 355,
where *mens* is *veritatis locus*.

17 See Ficino I, 363–4,343.

18 Ficino (I, 388) describes *ratio* as the proper species of *anima*, a mean
poised between the intelligible and material worlds.

19 III.ii.36. Exorcisms now give way to devotion to love's true fire, as in
III.iii.1–3, a prayer to love comparable in attitude to the *Hymns*.

20 See Jean Seznec, *The Survival of the Pagan Gods*, tr. Barbara F.
Sessions, Bollingen Series XXXVIII (New York, 1953), p. 137, for
Mantegna's Iliaco (Light): Cronico: Cosmico.

21 Wind, p. 44. Pseudo-Dionysius was much studied, translated, and
commented on by Renaissance Platonists. Among other possibilities
consider Ficino's triadic division of the human reason, closely con-
nected both with the theological virtues and with the *illuminari-
purgari-perfici* triad (I, 425); also his Light-Strength-Joy triad (I, 443),
which suggests a new perspective on the strong/weak moral schemes of
Faerie Queen II.

22 See Frank Kermode, 'The Cave of Mammon,' in *Elizabethan Poetry*,
Stratford-upon-Avon Studies 2 (London, 1960). My own 'The Image
of Mortality: *The Faerie Queene*, II. i–ii,' *Huntington Library Quar-
terly* 24 (1961), 'Emblems of Temperance in *The Faerie Queene*, Book
II,' *RES* 11 n.s. (1960), and 'The River Guyon,' *MLN* 75 (1960),
interpret Book II as a theological allegory of baptism, in which Guyon
is the cleansing river of Paradise, Gyon.

23 See Wind, p. 70n. and chaps. 3, 4 passim; also, on Pleasure as Psyche's
daughter, and on her place in the Neoplatonic divine *voluptas*, see
ibid., p. 62. Lexical frequencies confirm the existence of the triad:
perfect and its variants occur 17 times in Book III compared with 5
in Books I and II.

24 A danger not avoided by Maurice Evans in 'Platonic Allegory in *The Faerie Queene*,' *RES* 12 n.s. (1961), 132–43; particularly where he comes to the funny conclusion that 'Amoret, Britomart and Belphoebe form a trio which follows the pattern of Pulchritudo, Amor and Voluptas.'

25 See Wind, p. 42; also N.A. Robb, *Neoplatonism of the Italian Renaissance* (London, 1935).

26 Wind, p. 42, citing *Elements of Theology*, prop. 67. Cf. also prop. 139, *Elements*, ed. E.R. Dodds (Oxford, 1933), p. 254. As evidence of the currency of Proclus in Spenser's circle it may be worth mentioning that a fragment was translated by Ralegh (*The Poems of Sir Walter Ralegh*, ed. Agnes Latham, London, 1951, p. 59).

27 Lexical frequencies also show a preponderance of *fortune, chance,* and their variants in Book VI.

28 See Wind, p. 41.

29 Priscilla is restored to Aldus, Pastorella to Claribell, the bear's prey (by a white lie) to Matilda. On the fundamental triad, see Wind, p. 40. Lexical frequencies confirm the correspondence of VI with *remeatio*: thus *return* and its variants occur in Part 2 with the following frequencies: Book IV, 10 times; Book V, 13; Book VI, 22.

30 On the negative character of Fortuna in Book II see Harry Berger, *The Allegorical Temper* (New Haven, 1957), where the importance of this element is however exaggerated; see my review in *EC* 10 (1960), 338–9.

31 See Wind, p. 111.

32 On the Neoplatonic interpretations of the Graces, see ibid., esp. chaps 3 and 4.

33 This theme is well developed by Harry Berger in 'A Secret Discipline: *The Faerie Queene*, Book VI,' *Form and Convention in the Poetry of Edmund Spenser*, ed. William Nelson (New York and London, 1961), pp. 35–75.

34 This reading is preferred to 'froward' for the reasons given in Wind, p. 33, n. 3.

35 See Wind, p. 33 and chaps. 2–3 passim.

36 See ibid., p. 40, n. 5.

37 Ital. *dispetto*: despite, disdain, scorn.

38 Obviously Deception; but ironically also from Ital. *dicetto*, deceived – wily beguiled.

39 Perhaps punning between *difetto*, find fault, and *difetto*, fall short, give short measure. This ambiguity corresponds exactly to that in the third aspect of the Graces, discussed above.

40 Kathleen Williams, 'Courtesy and Pastoral in *The Faerie Queene*, Book VI,' *RES* 13 n.s. (1962), 345.

41 VI.ii.16,18; VI.iii.20–1.

42 'Courtesy and Pastoral,' p. 345.

43 Ficino, cit. in Wind, pp. 42–3.

44 See Russell A. Peck, 'Theme and Number in Chaucer's *Book of the Duchess*,' *Silent Poetry*, ed. Alastair Fowler (London, 1970), p. 93.

45 Besides the general intention (the golden mean), the face or fortified

wall of Medina may allude to the fort Medina in Malta, beleaguered by paynims such as Sansloy during the 1565 Siege of Malta. But I take for granted a domestic topical allegory in which Medina is the ecclesiastical *via media* headed by Elizabeth, between the puritanical reforming excess Huddibras and the libertine papist excess Sansloy.

46   The Letter to Ralegh discusses this procedure with respect to the last two images: 'For considering she [Elizabeth] beareth two persons, the one of a most royal Queen or Empress, the other of a most virtuous and beautiful Lady, this latter part in some places I do express in Belphoebe'; explaining it, in effect, in terms of the sovereign's two bodies, a legal doctrine itself implying the reality of an ideal world. See Ernst H. Kantorowicz, *The King's Two Bodies: A Study in Medieval Political Theology* (Princeton, 1957), cit. in Nelson, p. 124.

47   See Alastair Fowler, 'Oxford and London Marginalia to *The Faerie Queene*,' *N&Q* 206 (1961), 417.

48   *Memorabilia* III.10; cf. Aristotle, *Politics* 1281ᵇ. The notion found its way into the Renaissance stock of commonplaces; see, e.g., Roger Ascham, *English Works*, ed. W.A. Wright (Cambridge, 1904), p. 100.

49   Attention is drawn to this characteristic in Alastair Fowler, 'Six Knights at Castle Joyous,' *Studies in Philology* 56 (1959); Nelson, *Poetry of Edmund Spenser*; and Lewis, *Spenser's Images of Life*.

50   For the interpretations of the boar as chaos and as concupiscence, see Pierio Valeriano, *Hieroglyphica ... commentariorum libri lviii ... Accesserunt loco auctarii, hieroglyphicorum collectanea* (Frankfort, 1613), 68 D.

51   Perhaps cf. the pun on *overwrought* in De Quincey, *Reminiscences of the English Lake Poets*, ed. John E. Jordan (Everyman ed., London, 1907), p. 45.

52   On the symbolism of the glass globe of III.ii.20 (compared to Phao's brittle tower at III.ii.20), in which Britomart has her vision of Artegall, see Fowler, *Spenser and the Numbers of Time*, p. 124n. Cf. also vi.viii.42, where Serena's 'belly white and clear ... like an altar did it self uprear, / To offer sacrifice divine thereon.'

53   To leave the lists early was considered dishonourable: see Sir William Segar, *The book of honour and arms* (1590), pp. 73–5.

54   See Wind, pp. 81–8, where the history of the doctrine is traced, with special reference to the moderation of Venus and Mars. On good and evil forms of the same god in astrological thought, see, e.g., Raymond Klibansky et al., *Saturn and Melancholy* (London, 1964), pp. 251–2.

55   See Lewis, *Spenser's Images of Life*, pp. 82n., 135–6.

56   Angus Fletcher, *Allegory: The Theory of a Symbolic Mode* (Ithaca, NY, 1964), pp. 195 et passim.

57   Cit. in Nelson, *Poetry of Edmund Spenser*, p. 121.

58   See, e.g., ibid., p. 133: 'The narrative structure of *The Faerie Queene* is, in fact, almost frivolously weak.'

59   At II.vii.41–2, a passage sufficient in itself to show that Guyon's descent into the Cave is not without fault. He may be morally temperate, but he is disdainful, and therefore, presumably, spiritually proud.

60   I.ix.13ff. In spite of a possible allusion to the *Tale of Sir Thopas*, it is

quite unnecessary and inappropriate to suppose any comic intention. Spenser was well able to take an unfinished thread from Chaucer, as Ariosto from Boiardo, and work it in entirely to his own purpose (he does so again with *The Squire's Tale* and the Legend of Cambell and Triamond). The use of literary material in this way is really a kind of manneristic alienation effect, emphasizing the literary status of the fiction.

61 'Platonic Allegory in *The Faerie Queene*,' p. 132.
62 v.xii.37–43. Artegall is notably lacking in courteous finesse: one recalls his emblem 'Salvagesse sans finesse.'

Spenser *ludens*

WILLIAM NELSON

To Drayton's 'grave moral' and Milton's 'sage and serious' Spenser I would add, not altogether as a footnote, a playful one. The idea that whatever is comic about *The Faerie Queene* is so despite its author no doubt continues to prevail. Yet at least since the time of Upton some readers have been moved to laugh with Spenser rather than at him, and in recent years the response has been common enough to generate a number of essays with such titles as 'Spenser's High Comedy,' 'His Earnest unto Game: Spenser's Humor in *The Faerie Queene*,' 'Spenserian Humor: *Faerie Queene* III and IV,' and a doctoral dissertation called 'The Comedy of *The Faerie Queene*.'[1] It has even been proposed that mirthlessness is the quality not of the poet but of his scholarly commentators. Perhaps the wind is shifting.

I am indebted to these studies for many of the examples I shall cite. But I am concerned particularly with the kind of playfulness in which the player mocks his own role. Much of what is remarked as humorous in *The Faerie Queene* is an integral part of its fictional stuff. When, for example, Spenser makes fun of Braggadocchio or shows us those fair ladies vainly trying to put on the girdle of chastity the comedy arises within the story: the characters are ridiculed but the tale is not. I wish here to draw attention to Spenser's jesting, not at the characters and their actions, but at his own fiction, mockery deliberately designed to undermine the narrative illusion. The difference is that between our laughter at and with Falstaff, in whom we do believe, and our laughter at Chaucer's Sir Thopas, in whom we do not. Of course, *The Faerie Queene* is not an outright burlesque like the 'Tale of Sir Thopas.' But there is burlesque in it, and recognition of that quality should temper and refine our reading of the poem. I take as my text the comment of R.W. Church in the 'English Men of Letters' series: 'It has been said that Spenser never smiles. He not only smiles, with amusement or sly irony; he wrote what he must have laughed at as he wrote, and meant us to laugh at.'[2]

What he wrote was a heroic poem of high moral purpose, certainly not a laughing matter for the Renaissance. But it was also a narrative fiction dealing with brave knights' and ladies' gentle deeds, a tale typical of what Dean Colet called the 'blotterature' of ignorant and misguided ages. In the glow of Renaissance self-esteem, chivalric story was an absurd, dead fashion, worthy only of such mocking uses as Ariosto made of it. 'King Arthur's knights long since are fled,' wrote Thomas Howell in 1581.[3] Thomas Nashe described stories of this genre as 'the fantasticall dreames of those exiled Abbie-lubbers, from whose idle pens proceeded those worne out impressions of the feyned no where acts, of Arthur of the rounde table, Arthur of litle Brittaine, sir Tristram, Hewon of Burdeaux, the Squire of low degree, the foure sons of Amon, with infinite others.'[4] The editor of Spenser's *Shepheardes Calender* condemned the inventors of those 'no where acts' as 'fine fablers and lowd lyers.'[5] Ascham accused them of immorality, and Sidney's tutor warned against the reading of 'vile & blasphemous, or at lest of prophan and frivolous bokes, such as are that infamous legend of K. Arthur.'[6] Sidney himself was rather more indulgent, for in defence of fiction he argued that *Orlando Furioso* or 'honest King Arthur' would be more pleasing to a soldier than a discourse concerning the quiddity of *ens*.[7]

There was, certainly, a species of sub-literature in verse, in prose, and in the theatre which continued in all seriousness the tradition of the chivalric tale into the Renaissance and beyond. Its stubborn persistence in this kind is exemplified by the continuing popularity of *The Most Illustrious and Renowned History of the Seven Champions of Christendom*, the first part of which was first published in 1596.[8] I have an edition – it is called the eighteenth, which must be an understatement – printed in

Wilmington, Delaware, in 1804. It is in three parts, 'Containing their honourable Births, Victories, and noble Atchievements, by Sea and Land, in divers strange countries; their combats with Giants, Monsters, &c. Wonderful Adventures in Desarts, Wildernesses, inchanted Castles; their Conquests of Empires, Kingdoms; relieving distressed Ladies, with their faithful Loves to them: the Honor they won in Tilts and Tournaments, and success against the Enemies of Christendom.' The description is perfectly appropriate to the narrative of *The Faerie Queene*.

Spenser nevertheless elected this outmoded kind of story for his most ambitious undertaking. He had good reasons for doing so, some of which he lists himself. The example of Virgil taught him, as it taught Ronsard, to choose his hero from his nation's ancient past. Arthur's name was known to all, yet so little was recorded about him historically, particularly before his accession to the throne, that the poet was free to make fictions, precisely the activity that defined him as a poet. 'Fierce warres and faithfull loves' provided appropriate metaphors for the conflicts and attractions central to the moral problems with which he was concerned. And despite such mockery and abuse as I have cited, the chivalric tradition carried with it an atmosphere of golden antiquity, of 'beautiful old rhyme / In praise of ladies dead and lovely knights' (if not *The Faerie Queene* what could Shakespeare have been thinking of?). Samuel Daniel would have others 'sing of Knights and Palladines / In aged accents and untimely words: / Paint shadowes in imaginary lines / Which well the reach of their high wits records.'[9] Queen Elizabeth's Accession Day festivities continued to honour, at least ceremonially, the outworn ritual of tilt and tournament. In later centuries the influence of *The Faerie Queene* itself and the search for some equivalent of the moribund pastoral made of the tales of ladies, of knights and their impossible adventures a kind of golden literary world. But the ambivalence of Renaissance attitudes with respect to the chivalric tradition is illustrated dramatically in Shakespeare's *Troilus and Cressida* when noble Hector's storybook challenge to single combat for the honour of a fair lady provokes both admiration for a knightly gesture and Thersites' comment, 'Tis trash.'

Spenser is no Thersites, but he too recognizes the absurdity of chivalric narrative and from time to time exposes it to his own amusement and that of his readers. He confronts literary convention with the world as it is, not by means of guffaw, but by a subtle use of devices common to all burlesque – hyperbole, bathos, and patent illogic. That many passages in *The Faerie Queene* are hyperbolic, bathetic, and illogical, few would deny. The question remains, however, whether they are so because of the poet's naiveté or because of his sophistication. It is not a question that can be answered definitively, for it is not given to us to recapture fully the mood in which a work centuries old was written and read. Furthermore, the attempt to answer it is by its nature self-defeating, for all dissection injures its subject, and of all subjects literary tone must be the most delicate. And who has ever laughed at a dissected joke?

A test case may serve to focus the issue. In the course of the climactic battle between St George and the dragon, a battle fraught with the most profound moral and religious significance, the knight wounds his adversary under the wing: (1.xi.22)

> Forth flowed fresh
> A gushing river of blacke goarie blood,
> That drowned all the land, whereon he stood;
> The streame thereof would drive a water-mill.

In the Ovidian battle which Spenser appears to have been imitating the monster's hemorrhage merely dyes the grass red (*Metamorphoses* III, 85–6). Does Spenser's passage lie within the fictional convention of desperate encounters, so that the hyperbole of the bloody river and the incongruity of the water-mill are not parody but failure of taste, or is he mocking that convention at the same time as he makes use of it? If Chaucer were the author, the question would be easy to resolve. In the 'Knight's Tale' the sworn friends Palamon and Arcite agree to settle their competition for the love of Emily by mortal combat. They chivalrously arm each other and then chivalrously hack at each other. Perhaps this teeters on the boundary between fictional gallantry and burlesque of it. The story continues: (ll. 1660–2)

> Up to the ancle foghte they in hir blood.
> And in this wise I lete hem fightyng dwelle,
> And forth I wole of Theseus yow telle.

The blood tide is rather too high, the transition too abrupt. We are not disposed to take 'Up to the ancle foghte they in hir blood' as inept hyperbole because we know that Chaucer is neither stupid nor lacking in a sense of the absurd. Nor can we dismiss the 'Knight's Tale' as mere burlesque, like the 'Tale of Sir Thopas.' In the delicate balance that Chaucer achieves, the reader accepts the chivalric convention at the same time as he recognizes that from some points of view that convention is silly. But Spenser's reputation labours under those heavy Miltonic epithets. He is a self-confessed allegorist dedicated to a moral purpose, a method and end we have been taught to regard as grimly humourless. The contrast of *The Faerie Queene* with *Orlando Furioso* reinforces our prejudice: the English poet borrows episode and rhetoric from the Italian but not his mood, and sometimes he seems to miss or (as I think) to ignore Ariosto's jokes. We read the *Orlando* as a delicious Renaissance entertainment; because *The Faerie Queene* is so very different some critics are led to think of it as a late flowering of a decayed tradition rather than as a poem of the high Renaissance deliberately dressed in an outworn fashion.

In fact, much of Spenser's poetry is conceived as though it were by somebody else – as Harry Berger neatly puts it, written in quotation marks. The pompous lugubriousness of *The Teares of the Muses*, the rusticity of language and rudeness of rhythm of *The Shepheardes Calender*, the simplicity of the shepherds of *Colin Clouts Come Home Againe* are surely dramatically assumed poses. There is not, I think, any self-mockery in these; rather we are asked to admire the skill with which the poet plays his roles. In *Amoretti* the invented speaker is Spenser himself posing as conventional sonneteer. Louis Martz has remarked not only on the consciously artificial nature of that pose but also upon Spenser's subtle parody of it.[10] In Sonnet LIV, Martz points out, Spenser speaks directly of his playing diverse pageants in the world's theatre, and complains that whether he 'mask in myrth' or make his woes a 'tragedy' his lady merely mocks. Surely the reader is invited to react similarly – to mock, though not merely.

Among the many voices of *The Faerie Queene* is one which tells its story as though it were written by a poet of long ago, ancient and therefore good, simple, and credulous, a lover of the fair and the brave. Often he does not fully understand the meaning of the tale he tells; sometimes he distorts it. His language is marked by archaisms, his story by the clichés of mediaeval romance. He is not unlike the figure of the poet Gower whom Shakespeare puts forward as the 'presenter' of *Pericles* – that 'mouldy play' as Ben Jonson called it. Behind this poet-narrator stands Spenser himself, making his presence felt from time to time in order to remind the reader that he has only suspended his disbelief, that the tale of heroes and heroines, monsters and witches, however profound its significance may be, is nevertheless only a tale. This he does typically in those passages in which the story is most characteristically old-fashioned.

Among the most conspicuous features of mediaeval narrative is its pretence that it is indeed historically true, based upon authoritative documents or reports. Rabelais mocks this pretence in *Gargantua*, Boiardo and Ariosto in their *Orlandos*, More in *Utopia*, Cervantes in *Don Quixote*. Robert Durling remarks on humorous pseudo-documentation in Boiardo and Ariosto, but Spenser, he says, 'uses the mention of supposed sources of the poem ... to lend authority, plausibility, or an aura of antiquity to the story – never for humorous effect.'[11] Like most absolutes, I doubt that this one can be sustained. The key passage in which Spenser defends the historical truth of his story is the Prologue to Book II. As More had done before him, Spenser pretends to be disturbed by the idea that some readers may doubt his veracity,

> That all this famous antique history,
> Of some th'aboundance of an idle braine
> Will judged be, and painted forgery,
> Rather then matter of just memory.

He is forced to admit that the 'antiquities' he cites as authority are hard to come by. Yet the Amazon River and Virginia really were there before they were found, and other populated regions, perhaps even those in outer space, no doubt await other explorers. Therefore, he argues, Fairyland exists because it has not yet been discovered. The logical absurdity should warrant at least a smile.

Sometimes the reader is invited to verify the truth of the tale himself. Should he happen by the region of Merlin's cave (its location is precisely given though not easy to find) he must not attempt to enter its recesses 'For feare the cruell Feends should thee unwares devowre' (iii.iii.8). Rather, Spenser advises, he should put his ear to the ground so that he can hear the dreadful noises within. A similar effect is produced by the testimony to the historic reality of Arthur's sword. After Arthur's death, we are told, (i.vii.36)

> the Faerie Queene it brought
> To Faerie lond, where yet it may be seene, if sought.

Had the poet stopped with 'where yet it may be seene' the reader might well have taken it as the usual coin of chivalric narrative designed, as Durling suggests, to lend an aura of antiquity to the story. But the addition of 'if sought' must make him wonder how to go about the seeking.

No chivalric tale can properly be without its desperate encounters between knight and knight or knight and horrid beast. Sparks fly, armour plate is riven, blood flows in torrents. There are many such battles in *The Faerie Queene*, and C.S. Lewis thinks that Spenser does this kind of thing very badly.[12] But perhaps that usually admirable critic failed to distinguish between bad writing and something that verges on parody. I let pass the dragon's-blood-operated water-mill for some may think it seriously intended. But there can be no difference of opinion about Corflambo's recognition of his defeat by Arthur: (iv.viii.45)

> ere he wist, he found
> His head before him tombling on the ground ...

Or Artegall's conquest of Grantorto: (v.xii.23)

> Whom when he saw prostrated on the plaine,
> He lightly reft his head, to ease him of his paine ...

Or Britomart's overthrow of Sir Scudamour: (iv.vi.10)

> to the ground she smote both horse and man;
> Whence neither greatly hasted to arise,
> But on their common harmes together did devise ...

Or Radigund's escape from Artegall's huge stroke: (v.iv.41)

> had she not it warded warily,
> It had depriv'd her mother of a daughter ...

Or the desperate fight between that virago and Britomart: (v.vii.29)

> [they] spared not
> Their dainty parts, which nature had created
> So faire and tender, without staine or spot,
> For other uses, then they them translated;
> Which they now hackt and hewd, as if such use they hated.

Mocking the precision of a grocery clerk, Spenser says that the maw of the Blatant Beast has the capacity of 'A full good pecke within the utmost brim' (vi.xii.26). Orgoglio's yell of pain when Arthur cuts off his left arm is likened, oddly enough, to the bellow of a herd of sexually excited bulls (i. viii.11). A few stanzas after the amputation of that member the giant returns to the fray: (i.viii.18)

> The force, which wont in two to be disperst,
> In one alone left hand he now unites ...

Evidently Spenser is lightheartedly willing to undermine the seriousness of these combats even though they must signify the desperate struggles of the soul.

The most desperate of these is surely that of the Red Cross Knight against the powers that would destroy him. The subtle Archimago is a formidable magician indeed, capable of transforming himself into a dragon, of course, but also into fish, fowl, or fox, forms so terrifying (i.ii.10)

> That of himselfe he oft for feare would quake,
> And oft would flie away.

And the story of the final battle with the satanic dragon – that in which the water-mill passage occurs – is handled no more respectfully. If one wishes to find a prime example of the comparison of great things to small, there can be few more striking instances than the likening of the *well of life* which can restore the dead and wash away the guilt of sinful crime to the 'English *Bath*, and eke the german *Spau*' (I.xi.30). When the new-born knight rises from immersion in that well he wounds his adversary with his sword, hardened, Spenser suggests, by holy-water dew. The dragon, dazed and terribly angered, roars and renews the attack: (I.xi.37)

> Then gan he tosse aloft his stretched traine,
> And therewith scourge the buxome aire so sore,
> That to his force to yeelden it was faine.

The 'buxome' gives it away. No doubt the obedient air did yield, as it does to the tail of my kitten.

Other examples of what must be deliberate bathos and incongruity are easy to find. The cosmic challenge of Mutability to the principle of constancy in the world takes the form of a motion at law, so that the ruler of Olympus is constrained to bid Dan Phoebus (who here becomes court clerk) to 'Scribe her Appellation seale' (VII.vi.35). The list of 'idle fantasies' that flit in the chamber of Phantastes in the House of Alma includes supernatural beings, beasts, birds, and humans graded in anticlimax: (II.ix.50)

> Infernall Hags, *Centaurs*, feendes, *Hippodames*,
> Apes, Lions, Aegles, Owles, fooles, lovers, children, Dames.

The cannibal nation, having made captive the sleeping Serena, debate as to whether to eat her at once or let her sleep her fill, deciding on the latter course by cook-book logic: (VI.viii.38)

> For sleepe they sayd would make her battill better.

(To 'battill' means to fatten, as for the table.) When the naked girl is rescued at the critical moment by Sir Calepine, she says not a word to him. Her silence Spenser explains by describing her mood as 'unwomanly' (VI.viii.51). As for Calepine himself, since the great work by Calepino was so well known to all Europe that his name had become a common noun, he must have meant 'dictionary' or 'thesaurus' to Spenser's reader, rather more specifically than 'Webster' does to us. I do not quite get the force of this joke, but it must be a joke because among the other characters in this sixth book are Aldus and his son Aldine, as who should say, The Clarendon Press.

Story-book ladies are of course incomparably beautiful, and Spenser's are no exception. Since the poet tells us that in some places Belphoebe shadows the Queen herself, the highest reach of praise is called for. Yet, as Watkins remarks,[13] it may be even beyond that reach to say that the double pleasure of sight and smell provided by the roses and lilies of Belphoebe's face is (II.iii.22)

Hable to heale the sicke, and to revive the ded.

A few stanzas later in this blazon the hyperbolic mood is suddenly broken: (II.iii.27)

Below her ham her weed did somewhat traine ...

I am not absolutely sure about that 'ham.' Its primary meaning is 'the back of the knee' and Spenser uses the word again in describing the way the Amazon Radigund tucks up her dress in order to free herself for action. Still, it is not a word one expects to find in an encomium on the beauty of so noble a lady as Belphoebe.[14] And what is one to make of Spenser's choice of simile for her legs: (II.iii.28)

Like two faire marble pillours they were seene,
Which doe the temple of the Gods support,
Whom all the people decke with girlands greene,
And honour in their festivall resort ...

The marble pillars derive from the Song of Solomon, but the bedecked temple which they support appears to be Spenser's addition. The comparison is only less curious than that produced for Serena's 'goodly thighes': (VI.viii.42)

whose glorie did appeare
Like a triumphall Arch, and thereupon
The spoiles of Princes hang'd, which were in battel won.

No doubt the poet wished to suggest the awe-struck admiration which the sight of those legs and thighs would arouse. But if the descriptions were written in all seriousness would he have made these visions so ceremonially public?

Jests based on physiological function and so-called 'kitchen' subjects seem particularly inappropriate for so elevated a discourse as *The Faerie Queene*. The reference to the natural uses of the dainty parts of Britomart and Radigund is therefore startling, but it is not unique. A comprehensive anatomy of the House of Soul must inevitably include a description of its service rooms, but the kitchen of this generally well ordered establishment seems to me so volcanically overheated as to require radical remedy: (ii.ix.29)

> in the midst of all
> There placed was a caudron wide and tall,
> Upon a mighty furnace, burning whot,
> More whot, then *Aetn'*, or flaming *Mongiball* ...

And the section devoted to this digestive subject ends with puns not demanded by Spenser's moral purpose: (ii.ix.32)

> all the rest, that noyous was, and nought,
> By secret wayes, that none might it espy,
> Was close convaid, and to the back-gate brought,
> That cleped was *Port Esquiline*, whereby
> It was avoided quite, and throwne out privily.

Even the daintiest of story-book ladies, Spenser reminds us, must on occasion suffer just such inconveniences as ordinary people do. Britomart having fallen asleep, the lovely Amoret leaves the security of her protector's martial prowess and (iv.vii.4)

> Walkt through the wood, for pleasure, or for need ...

There is nothing inherently funny about the circumstance that Amoret should 'for need' go off into the woods. The joke is at the expense not of the girl but of the narrative illusion itself – the fictional lady is here confronted by one with the usual complement of digestive organs. Here, and in the other passages I have been citing, what is within the fictional frame is faced directly or implicitly by what is without. The result is not as catastrophic as the confrontation of the Snowy Florimell by the true one. The fiction does not melt away as the snow lady does; rather it stands revealed for what it is, attention having been drawn to the fact that it is an illusion. However improper critics may find such effects – Henry James thought such betrayals 'a terrible crime' – story-tellers not infrequently seek them. Shakespeare is so bold as to remind his audience that the actor playing the part of Polonius is not Polonius at all but the actor who once played the part of Julius Caesar – at a London theatre, surely, rather than at the university of the fiction. There may be a parallel in a kind of Persian painting in which an equestrian scene is surrounded by a painted frame into which intrude the tail and hoof of one of the horses. The frame so emphasized identifies the scene as an artistic conception and so divides it from real life. But at the same time as the intrusion of hoof and tail denies the reality of the artistic conception it underscores its relevance to the large real world outside.

Overt jests at the expense of the fiction are not to be found in every stanza or in every canto of *The Faerie Queene*. They are nevertheless common enough to warn the reader that the naiveté of the narrator is a deliberately assumed pose, that Spenser is playing a part and expects his audience to know it. Nowhere does this mock-naiveté appear more strikingly than in the story which is formally (though in form only) the principal action of the whole poem, the enamourment of Prince Arthur and his quest for Gloriana, Queen of the Fairies (i.ix.8–15). If Spenser was to assume the role of an ancient story-teller, what better choice of tale could he make than one so old-fashioned that Chaucer made fun of himself by telling it? Arthur's resemblance to the absurd Sir Thopas is unmistakable. Both chastely reject love; both on a day ride out hunting. Arthur is 'prickt forth with jollitie / Of looser life'; Thopas pricks forth both north and east and falls into a love-longing. For Arthur all nature laughs; for Thopas the herbs spring and the birds sing. Both weary of their sportful pricking and dismount to lie down on the soft grass. Arthur uses his helmet as a pillow, an uncomfortable practice which Chaucer tells us (though not in the immediate context) is also Thopas's. The Prince dreams that the Queen of Fairies lies down beside him and makes him 'Most goodly glee and lovely blandishment.' Sir Thopas has a similar dream: a fairy queen shall be his leman and lie beneath his cloak. On waking both heroes resolve to find their dream loves and their search takes them both to the country of Faery. And nothing more is heard of either quest. Though both poems are aborted, surely for different reasons, each has room for development of the story but neither makes use of it. In Spenser's version Chaucer's tail rhyme – 'drasty ryming' (as the Host calls it) – is turned into the Spenserian stanza; obvious banalities are eliminated. Yet although the new version surely signifies the seductive power upon noble youth of a dream of glory, the story itself remains puerile, the characters unrealized, the events barely recounted, their sequence unmotivated. Since we recognize the similarity of the tale of Arthur's dream to that of Sir Thopas many of Spenser's contemporaries must also have recognized it.

For some modern readers it is intolerable to believe that the central action of a poem of such manifest seriousness as *The Faerie Queene* could derive from a patent joke. Yet Spenser not only read 'Sir Thopas' but he read it attentively, for he refers to Thopas and the giant Ollyphant elsewhere in his poem, and in his treatise on Ireland he discourses learnedly, though no doubt erroneously, on the resemblance of Thopas's costume to the dress of Irish horsemen.[15] One scholar attempts to resolve the dilemma by suggesting that Spenser took Chaucer's tale in dead earnest; lacking humour himself he found no humour in it. Another concludes that since 'Thopas' is funny, Spenser's source must have been some other mediaeval story, no doubt one of the kind that Chaucer burlesques. Yet another argues that since the tale of Arthur's enamourment plainly derives from 'Sir Thopas' it must be the residue of an earlier draft of *The Faerie Queene*, one without pretensions to didactic purpose and written at the time Spenser was proposing to overgo Ariosto rather than to fashion a gentleman or noble person in virtuous and gentle discipline. But it is inconceivable that any normally intelligent adult could take Chaucer's story seriously, almost as inconceivable as that a scholar should think that he did. Similar tales are of course to be found in mediaeval literature – why else should Chaucer have ridiculed them? – but Spenser had no need to seek elsewhere for his matter. And whether or not the story of Arthur's falling in love and vowing his great quest is part of the debris of an earlier version of *The Faerie Queene*, the poet did include it in the work which he presented so proudly to Queen Elizabeth. If narrative of this kind is what Gabriel Harvey objected to when he described that draft of the poem that Spenser sent him in 1580 as '*Hobgoblin* runne away with the Garland from *Apollo*' the criticism still holds for the work as we have it. Spenser's imitation of the Thopas story, coupled with his mocking use of the clichés of chivalric narrative, leads to the conclusion that he found nothing incompatible in the association of an absurd tale and a deeply moral significance.

As Curtius shows, the Middle Ages did not doubt that jest and earnest could live together.[16] Prudentius finds it appropriate for St Lawrence on the gridiron to suggest to his executioners that since he has been cooked on one side they have the opportunity of deciding whether the rare or the well-done is more savoury. Hagiographers enliven their accounts of the saints with reports of how they miraculously make broken bottles whole or end a plague of insects by excommunicating them. In heroic poetry, too, comedy had its licence, given authority by Servius's judgment that the story of Dido in the fourth book of the *Aeneid* is almost wholly comic in style, naturally, says Servius, since its subject is love. To Curtius's mediaeval examples I would add a Renaissance one: the episode in Canto ix of Camoens's *Lusiads* which concerns the delicious isle on which Thetys and her nubile nymphs provide sexual reward for the comically eager sailors of Vasco da Gama's heroic expedition. Camoens explains at last that the isle is not an isle and the nymphs not nymphs: (ix.89)[17]

> 'For these fair Daughters of the Ocean,
> 'Thetys and the Angellick pensil'd Isle,
> 'Are nothing but sweet Honour, which These wan;
> 'With whatsoever makes a life not vile.
> 'The priviledges of the Martial Man,
> 'The Palm, the Lawrell'd Triumph, the rich spoile;
>   'The Admiration purchac't by his sword;
>   'These are the joys, this Island doth afford.

The equation of sexual satisfaction with 'sweet Honour' and 'Lawrell'd Triumph' is exactly that of Arthur's dream of Gloriana.

Such disparity between story and meaning goes against the modern grain. We have been taught by the Aristotelian doctrine that plot is the soul of a tragedy or epic poem, out of which we derive the notion that there should be a community of mood between the tale and such significance as it may have. Our sense of the nature of fiction has developed from the tradition of the novel and its central tendency of 'formal realism' as Ian Watt calls it. Once we have opened the pages of a novel we do not wish to be reminded that we are within its frame, that the events recorded are not true history. For the space of our reading we expect to be captivated, to find the characters 'convincing,' the plot (however fantastic) within its terms believable. So Watt, for example, judges Fielding's ironic attitude towards the reality of his characters a grave fault; no doubt he finds Nabokov's tone similarly blameworthy. Much of the harshest criticism of *The Faerie Queene* arises from such novel-bred expectations. Spenser's stories do not hang together very well, narrative threads are left untied, episodes succeed each other apparently at haphazard, characters lack recognizable humanity. To counter such charges one apologist invokes a theory of successive careless revisions. Another attempts to discover a formal dramatic structure in the text, a construction I doubt it will bear. Yet another accounts for the inconsequence of the narrative by describing *The Faerie Queene* as a dream poem, and indeed the story has the apparent formlessness of a dream without the excuse that its maker is asleep. Some single out Britomart as truly flesh and blood, usually on the ground that she undergoes a jealous tantrum, but I am not convinced for all that that she is tangible. *The Faerie Queene* is not of the genre of *Pamela*, *War and Peace*, or even Tolkien's *Lord of the Rings*.

The skilful making of fictions is now held in high regard, but its estimation in the Renaissance was rather more equivocal. A strong current of critical theory did honour such invention as the very activity that identified the poet, distinguished him from the professors of other disciplines, and asserted his claim to the god-like title of 'maker.' But a story which simulates true history is a lie. When it is told with intent to deceive it is criminal; without such intent it becomes in common Renaissance opinion a kind of play, harmless and perhaps even recreative, but inevitably tainted with frivolity. Story reading is justifiable, therefore, for those whom nature or circumstance renders incapable of serious affairs: the very young and the very old, the traveller, the bedridden, the lady unencumbered by household duties; for such it provides solace and escape from the sin of sloth. Even Sidney, for whom poetry is the noblest of secular disciplines and fiction the heart of poetry, seems to share this view. The tales of his poet hold *children* from play and *old men* from the chimney corner, and, Sidney continues, it is the persistent childishness in mature men that makes them so receptive to imagined story. He describes his own *Arcadia* as 'no better stuffe, then, as in an Haberdashers shoppe, glasses or feathers.' William Painter says of his collection of novelle: 'Pleasaunt they be, for that they recreate, and refreshe weried mindes, defatigated either with painefull travaile, or with continuall care, occasioning them to shunne and avoid heavinesse of minde, vaine fantasies, and idle cogitations.' And Spenser himself half apologizes for his adoption of a narrative method to accomplish his moral purpose, urging his critics to be 'satisfide with the use of these dayes, seeing all things accounted by their showes, and nothing esteemed of, that is not delightfull and pleasing to commune sence.' The task of reconciling the merely recreative and therefore trivial character of fiction with the high moral aims of poetry is one of the principal concerns of Renaissance critical theory.

The sense that there is something childish about invented story is evident, I think, in some of the notable fictions of the age. Typically, the author of Renaissance story seems to stand apart from his tale, dissociating himself as it were from responsibility for it. 'Formal realism' is conspicuously absent, though virtuoso passages of vivid description – rhetorical *enargeia* – are often attempted. Those who find signs of nascent realism in fictions dealing with low or merchant life often mistake setting for kind, for such stories as *Lazarillo de Tormes*, *Jack Wilton*, and the Deloney novels are no more probable than *Arcadia* or *L'Astrée*. Parody is common: Ariosto and Cervantes mock the chivalric tradition, Erasmus the rhetorical, Rabelais the stories of giants, Thomas More the travellers' tales. None of these is merely parody, and in all but the *Orlando* the light fiction is made to carry a burden of weighty matter. This did not seem to trouble contemporary readers but it does confuse modern ones: the debate continues as to whether *The Praise of Folly, Utopia, Gargantua,* and *Don Quixote* are witty entertainments or grave discourses. Apparently the combination of jest and earnest is no longer congenial to us, or perhaps we are reluctant to grant the necessary sophistication to writers and audiences of the past.

The parodic quality in the narrative of the *Faerie Queene* is quite different from that of *Orlando Furioso.* Unlike Spenser's poem, Ariosto's could never be misunderstood, even by the dullest reader, for a straightforward example or imitation of the traditions it burlesques. Spenser's reader is indeed absorbed, as the poet himself claims to be, by that delightful land of Faery. But it can be delightful only if he does not really believe in those awful monsters, witches, and bloody combats. So from time to time he is nudged awake, though only tentatively, for the transitions are almost imperceptible, the narrative flow resumes, and the wounded illusion heals itself. Those moments should suffice, I think, to remove him just so far from the fiction that he is at once seduced by it and amused by his own seduction. Perhaps such a mood is set by the deliberately quaint 'pricking' and 'yclad' of the very first lines of the first canto. If the play of diction is so responded to, the reader will not trouble to inquire how that poor lamb kept pace with the Red Cross Knight and Una, nor will he feel inclined to suppose that since it is never seen again Una must have cooked it for supper.

NOTES

1   Among recent studies which discuss Spenser's humour at some length in one or another of its aspects are the following: Harry Berger, 'Spenser's "Faerie Queene," Book 1: Prelude to Interpretation,' *Southern Review: An Australian Journal of Literary Studies* 2:1 (1966), 18–49; Judith Petterson Clark, 'His Earnest unto Game: Spenser's Humor in "The Faerie Queene," ' *The Emporia State Research Studies: Medieval and Renaissance Studies* 15:4 (1967), 13–24, 26–7; Martha Craig, 'The Secret Wit of Spenser's Language,' in *Elizabethan Poetry,* ed. Paul Alpers (New York, 1967), pp. 447–72; Judith Dundas, 'Allegory as a Form of Wit,' *Studies in the Renaissance*

11 (1964), 223–33; Robert O. Evans, 'Spenserian Humor: *Faerie Queene* III and IV,' *Neuphilologische Mitteilungen* 60 (1959), 288–99; A.H. Gilbert, 'Spenserian Comedy,' *Tennessee Studies in Literature* 2 (1957), 95–104; Clyde G. Wade, *The Comedy of 'The Faerie Queene,'* unpublished doctoral dissertation, University of Missouri, Columbia, Missouri, 1967 (*Dissertation Abstracts* 28, 3651–2A); W.B.C. Watkins, *Shakespeare and Spenser* (Princeton, 1950), Note 1: 'Spenser's High Comedy (*Faerie Queene* 2. 3),' pp. 293–304; Arnold Williams, *Flower on a Lowly Stalk* (Michigan State University Press, 1967), pp. 113–20. An unpublished and undated essay on the subject by Charles Bell Burke is preserved at the library of the University of Tennessee. The first chapter of a projected book to be entitled 'The Comic Element in Spenser,' it surveys in considerable detail the opinions of Spenser's critics regarding his sense of humour, or lack of it. Burke expected to complete his work by October 1935. Burke did publish a note entitled 'The "Sage and Serious" Spenser,' *Notes and Queries* 175 (1938), 457–8.

2   *Spenser* (1st ed. 1879; London, 1906), p. 141.

3   Quoted in Charles Bowie Millican, *Spenser and the Table Round* (Cambridge, Mass., 1932), p. 183, from *Howell His Deuises* (1581).

4   *The Anatomie of Absurditie*, in *The Works of Thomas Nashe*, ed. Ronald B. McKerrow (Oxford, 1958), I, 11.

5   'April' gloss.

6   Quoted in Josephine Waters Bennett, *The Evolution of 'The Faerie Queene'* (Chicago, 1942), p. 75, from Nathaniel Baxter's dedication to his translation of Calvin's *Sermons* (1578).

7   *An Apology for Poetry*, ed. Geoffrey Shepherd (London, 1965), p. 127.

8   *STC* 14677.

9   *Delia*, Sonnet XLVI.

10   'The "Amoretti": "Most Goodly Temperature," ' *Form and Convention in the Poetry of Edmund Spenser*, Selected Papers from the English Institute, ed. William Nelson (New York, 1961), pp. 146–68.

11   *The Figure of the Poet in Renaissance Epic* (Cambridge, Mass., 1965), p. 224.

12   *The Allegory of Love* (Oxford, 1936), p. 347.

13   *Shakespeare and Spenser*, p. 300.

14   Shakespeare uses the word in *Romeo and Juliet* II.iv.57, *Hamlet* II.ii.203, and *Pericles* IV.ii.114, always in reference to men and always in derogation.

15   *A View of the Present State of Ireland*, ll. 2177ff.

16   *European Literature and the Latin Middle Ages*, trans. W.R. Trask (New York, 1953), Excursus IV.

17   Fanshawe's translation.

Our new poet:
Spenser, 'well of English undefyld'

A.C. HAMILTON

Allegorical interpretation is the art of telling 'stretchers.' Accordingly, the case against interpretation of *The Faerie Queene* is formidable. I have presented it in part in an article on modern critical approaches to the poem: 'For a poem which is such an elaborate dance of meanings, it becomes clear very quickly that interpretation is a matter of saying what the poem chooses not to say, and certainly not in the critic's words, or making explicit what the poem prefers to keep implicit. It forces a reading which the work obstinately resists or withholds for the moment of its own choosing ... All interpretation violates the poem's subtlety, complexity, and wholeness by rationalizing its imaginative statements. It seems designed to protect us from fearful exposure to the work itself ... Once criticism has brought an informed reader to the poem, it should leave him alone. As much may be said for any imaginative work, but it needs to be said with special emphasis for allegory whose images depend upon the responses that they awaken in readers, and above all for Spenser's allegory whose end is not understanding but virtuous action. *The Faerie Queene* is not meant to be understood but to be possessed. We look for moral meaning when we should be attending to released moral energy.'[1] I do not wish to press this case further except to stress, for my immediate purpose in this paper, that interpretation juggles words out of context. It selects its words by examining the poem through opaque filters – usually moral ones that come only in shades of grey – which allow only certain words to pass through, dim and distorted. After these words are associated with some analogous use in selected non-poetic contexts, they are put back into the poem; but now they are infected, being drained of poetic vitality and charged with non-poetic meaning.

I cannot recall any interpretation of *The Faerie Queene* which may not be faulted as a partial and distorted image of the poem. I am not thinking of perverse readings which offer a new view of the poem by turning it upside down but rather of those which all of us would accept as persuasive. For example, when the Red Cross Knight is defeated by Orgoglio, it seems reasonable to infer that he falls through pride. Most certainly he falls: one who was on horseback lies upon the ground, first to rest in the shade and then to lie with Duessa; although he staggers to his feet, he soon falls senseless upon the ground; and finally, he is placed deep underground in the Giant's dungeon. The Giant himself is not 'identified' until after the Knight's fall: then he is not named Pride but rather Orgoglio, a very un-English and un-pronounceable name. Though he is a proud giant, his pride is only one detail in a very complex description. In his size, descent, features, weapon, gait, and mode of fighting, he is seen as a par-ticular giant: he is not seen as a particular kind of pride. To name him Pride is to select a few words – and not particularly interest-ing ones – such as 'arrogant' and 'presumption' out of some twenty-six lines or about two hundred words, and to weight these as pride from their significance in theology. If then we say that the Knight falls through Pride, we interpret the episode perhaps to the satisfaction of most readers but we have left the poetry altogether. While the Knight is guilty of sloth and lust before he falls, he is not proud; in fact, he has just escaped from the House of Pride. At this point the interpreter may be tempted to ignore Orgoglio altogether and say simply that the Knight falls through lust. Then the sin of concupiscence supplies the basis for a re-ligious reading of the episode. Yet Spenser prevents any direct religious reading – he deliberately prevents it – by attributing the Knight's weakness before Orgoglio to his act of drinking, in ignorance, the enfeebling waters issuing from a nymph who, like him, rested in the middle of her quest.

My immediate quarrel with interpretation, however, is not that it remains abstract, generalized, and unfocused, but that it engages too little of the poem too obliquely and always at two removes from its 'Idea or fore-conceit.' It engages too few words in the poem, and even these it reads out of context. Interpretation may be controlled and refined by reading the words more carefully in context. The canto that relates the Knight's fall begins:

What man so wise, what earthly wit so ware,
As to descry the crafty cunning traine,
By which deceipt doth maske in visour faire,
And cast her colours dyed deepe in graine,
To seeme like Truth.

Since these lines seem to provide no more than a very general moral comment upon what follows, the reader is tempted to hurry over them. Yet he should pause because some words call attention to themselves within the context of the poem. For example, 'traine' signifies 'guile' but also the robe in which Duessa, the daughter of Deceit, is disguised. Duessa 'cast[s] her colours' in the sense in which that term is used in rhetoric and also in painting: she 'arranged her colours.' Yet the phrase means also 'to lose colour,' for Duessa, 'clad in scarlot red' (ii.13), appears in Una's 'visour faire.' Yet her colours are 'dyed deepe in graine' both in the general sense, 'dyed thoroughly,' and in the particular sense, 'dyed scarlet.' The care and precision with which these words are used should alert the reader to an awareness that each word and action may be significant: the Knight rests, he rests by a fountain, he is disarmed, his armour is rejected as 'yron-coted Plate,' his steed feeds, he feeds upon the shade – and so throughout the canto.

The significance of the words in the poem is defined by the language of allegory which Spenser employs. That the Knight 'feedes upon the cooling shade' and bathes his forehead in the wind which plays through 'the trembling leaves' recalls in general terms Jeremiah's denunciation of the sinner who lay down like a harlot under every tree that had green leaves. However, the meaning of these words is defined specifically by the similar setting of Fradubio's story of his fall (ii.28) and later by the Giant's entrance at which 'trees did tremble' (vii.7). Further, the acts of feeding upon the shade of the tree and of drinking the poisoned water become a prelude to the Knight's defeat by Orgoglio as later his feeding upon the Tree of Life and drinking from the Well of Life become a prelude to his victory over the Dragon. Spenser's language of allegory demands that one read the poem with the same care with which it was written. When its grammar is mastered, more words may be included in our response. For example, any reader should be prepared to respond to the careful wordplay in the lines that describe the Knight and Duessa as they 'bathe in pleasaunce of the joyous shade, / Which shielded them against the boyling heat' (vii.4). The use of that very Spenserian term 'pleasaunce' has been restricted to the kind of pleasure that the Knight first took with Duessa when he made 'faire seemely pleasaunce' (ii.30) with her under Fradubio's shade, and to the activity in the House of Pride when Lucifera's crew fed 'with pleasaunce of the breathing fields' (iv.38). The fact that the shade – 'joyous shade' is an oxymoron – now shields him infers the loss of his true shield of faith and so points to his present helplessness before 'the destruction that wasteth at noon day' (Psalm 91:6).

In the article quoted earlier I noted that modern criticism is 'moving to the point where each word bears an equal weight of significance.' The reviewer in the *Times Literary Supplement* termed such criticism 'a nightmare vision.' However, I approve its direction though I would claim that all words are equal in Orwell's sense: 'All words are equal but some words are more equal than others.' Ideally one should respond wholly to the poem by responding to it as a whole. In practice critics short-circuit much of it in order to assert some prose summary of meaning. Unfortunately, *The Faerie Queene* may be read all too easily on a number of allegorical levels. It remains very difficult to read on its literal level: then one must respond not to what it may be taken generally to mean but to what its words actually say. Most readers, at least most critics, forsake the golden words for drab ideas. In place of that maker who offers 'the brightnesse of brave and glorious words,'[2] we have substituted the philosopher/ thinker/church adherent who is the product of the Renaissance and Reformation (that was yesterday) or the 'sage and serious teacher' who is a severely Miltonic Spenser (that is today).

Spenser as a poet, the skilled craftsman in words, has hardly been understood. He deserves the praise which Jonson threw away on Coryate: 'he is a great and bold Carpenter of words, or (to expresse him in one like his owne) a Logodaedale.'
In his art of language Spenser is closer to the fabulous artificer Joyce than he is to the allegorist Dante. He shares Yeats's faith that 'Words alone are certain good'; he believes with Wallace Stevens that 'the gaiety of language is our seigneur'; and above all, he practises the craftsmanship of words upheld by Dylan Thomas:

> I am a painstaking, conscientious, involved and devious craftsman in words ... I use everything and anything to make my poems work and move in the directions I want them to: old tricks, new tricks, puns, portmanteau-words, parodox, allusion, paranomasia, paragram, catachresis, slang, assonantal rhymes, vowel rhymes, sprung rhythm. Every device there is in language is there to be used if you will. Poets have got to enjoy themselves sometimes, and the twistings and convolutions of words, the inventions and contrivances, are all part of the joy that is part of the painful, voluntary work.[3]

These verbal devices and many others are exploited by Spenser with the result that *The Faerie Queene* illustrates and justifies Sidney's daring claim that the English language is 'indeed capable of any excellent exercising of it.'[4]

In this paper I intend to consider the range and variety of Spenser's verbal craftsmanship: his care and precision in choice of words, his use of etymology and puns, his use of ambiguity in syntax and meanings of words, and his word-coinages. Since his art of language is sophisticated, complex, and immensely varied, I restrict myself to a general survey and cite only representative examples from the poem. My subject remains largely unexplored and my remarks are merely suggestive.

The general meaning of a word in its poetic context may be clarified through spelling or etymology, its place in the line, its relation to other words in the line and stanza, and its thematic use in the canto or book. For most words one need note only the care and precision with which they are used to reveal their meanings. For example, after Guyon leaves Phaedria's island and before he meets Mammon, he is compared to a mariner: (II.vii.1–2)

> As Pilot well expert in perilous wave,
>   That to a stedfast starre his course hath bent,
>   When foggy mistes, or cloudy tempests have
>   The faithfull light of that faire lampe yblent,
>   And cover'd heaven with hideous dreriment,
>   Upon his card and compas firmes his eye,
>   The maisters of his long experiment,
>   And to them does the steddy helme apply,
> Bidding his winged vessell fairely forward fly:
>
> So *Guyon* having lost his trusty guide,
>   Late left beyond that *Ydle lake*, proceedes
>   Yet on his way, of none accompanide;
>   And evermore himselfe with comfort feedes,
>   Of his owne vertues, and prayse-worthy deedes.

These lines serve usefully enough as filler between two major episodes in Guyon's journey. The simile itself is too traditional to call attention to itself. Only through reading the rest of the poem may the reader appreciate and understand its use here, and recognize, for example, its special relevance to the Knight of Temperance whose mastery over the passions is expressed as a victory over water. The phrase, 'a stedfast starre,' may be taken to refer to 'the stedfast starre' (I.ii.1) which, as the curious reader may note, is Arcturus, that star associated with Arthur who guides each knight. However, the indefinite article controls any larger inference here. The balanced phrases 'faithfull light' and 'faire lampe' express the love of light and horror of darkness which extend throughout the poem, again without any special point here except as Guyon is about to enter the darkness of Mammon's cave. The term 'dreriment' would strike any reader as particularly Spenserian: its general meanings, whatever they are, are felt rather than understood, and made sufficiently explicit by the re-enforcing adjective 'hideous.' The first word that needs any gloss for a modern reader is 'card,' which refers to the mariner's geographical chart rather than the graduated compass card; and the first phrase that needs any explication is 'maisters of his long experiment' which means 'instruments of his long experience.' Yet for the sixteenth-century reader neither word or phrase would cause any difficulty. Even for the modern reader, the import of the two lines in which they occur is clear: as the mariner must turn from sure, heavenly guidance to his own, less reliable means, so Guyon must turn from the sure, outward guidance of the Palmer to his own inner virtue. In the ninth line the alliteration of 'f' in 'fairely forward fly' communicates a sense of speed – a dangerous speed – as it comes at the end of the stanza, but its use here as a verbal device is not obtrusive. In the next stanza the 'comfort' that Guyon finds in his own virtue has a precise sixteenth-century sense, 'aid, support' (OED 1); it lacks entirely the modern sense of 'moral smugness' (which it seems to arouse in Guyon's modern readers). 'In this time, place, and fortune,' Sidney's two princes say in a similar moment of crisis, 'it is lawful for us to speak gloriously.' The entire phrase, 'with comfort feedes, / Of his owne vertues,' reveals both the self-sufficiency by which Guyon may resist Mammon's temptations and the limitations of his virtue. As he feeds upon his virtues, he confronts Mammon who 'feede[s] his eye' (4) upon gold, and is led into a realm where he too 'did feed his eyes' (24) upon Mammon's riches. By the end of the temptation, he has consumed his own virtues, faints through lack of food, and lies helpless before his enemies. The fuller import of the simile that opens canto vii is realized only in canto viii: heavenly powers must guide the Palmer to Guyon's side, and the Palmer, in turn, guides Arthur to uphold his side in the quarrel with Pyrochles and Cymochles. Only then does Guyon regain that sure, outward guidance which will carry him successfully on his voyage to the Bower of Bliss. In that final voyage the Palmer's staff and helmsman's stiff oars comment upon the 'card and compas' – notoriously unreliable means of navigation in the sixteenth century – to which his virtue may only be compared at the mid-point of his quest. Though these opening lines continually expand in significance through their context, their meaning is sufficiently clear in themselves. In these lines, then, and generally throughout the poem – though a poem of 36,000 lines – words are chosen with scrupulous care for their clarity and precision.

Any word or phrase that is repeated justifies the attention called to it. It does so because the whole poem possesses the harmonious unity of a dance. For example, when Guyon confronts Acrasia in her Bower, he binds her and 'their gardins did deface' (ii.xii.83). To many modern readers it has seemed that Guyon suddenly loses his cool and over-reacts. Yet that painful word 'deface,' with its implication of a wanton destruction of beauty, suggests how carefully Spenser articulates the concluding action of Book ii. As Arthur had confronted Maleger whose forces almost 'deface' (xi.6) the Castle of Alma until he, in response, 'fowle / Maleger doth deface' (xi.Argument), so Guyon confronts Acrasia whose lover 'his nobility [doth] so foul deface' (xii.79) and, imitating Arthur in his response, 'their gardins did deface.' With larger scope, repetition may be expressed through comparable actions within an episode and beyond it to include a whole book. For example, when Gardante wounds Britomart with his arrow, (iii.i.65)

> yet was the wound not deepe,
> But lightly rased her soft silken skin,
> That drops of purple bloud thereout did weepe,
> Which did her lilly smock with staines of vermeil steepe.

Immediately this description suggests Adonis's wound shown in the tapestry in the house of Malecasta: 'the gore, / Which staines his snowy skin with hatefull hew' (38). Love's wounding is shown to afflict all characters in the book. In the next canto the origin of her wound by Gardante is explained: she has been wounded by love through the sight of Artegall in Venus's glass (ii.24ff.). At the end of the book she receives a similar wound from Busyrane: (xii.33)

> it strooke into her snowie chest,
> That little drops empurpled her faire brest ...
> Albe the wound were nothing deepe imprest.

The curious word 'imprest,' which means imprinted, indicates that Busyrane marks in her flesh the characters which he writes with Amoret's blood in order to enchant her. This word is one of several designed to show how Britomart submits herself to Amoret's torture. She forces Busyrane to 'reherse' (36) the bloody verses that charm Amoret, that is, say over again what he had said to her. Upon hearing his verses, 'horror gan the virgins hart to perse' (36) just as Amoret's heart had been pierced. Through her chastity, however, she triumphs. Such repetition suggests that Amoret embodies Britomart's love for Artegall. Further, it clarifies Britomart's role in Book III. While the Red Cross Knight defeats his enemy by force and Guyon his by wit, she triumphs by submitting herself as a sacrifice. By closely attending to such a simple device as verbal repetition, the reader is led to understand the allegory.

Scrupulous care and precision in choice of words mark any major poet. Among them Spenser is distinguished as a Renaissance poet by his witty use of words; and among Renaissance poets he is distinguished by his joy in words. Only Shakespeare in *Love's Labour's Lost* matches him. He was sustained to write the longest major poem in our language because words released in him enormous creative powers. He seems never to tire. After the lengthy procession of rivers, which may exhaust the attention of the most sympathetic reader, he continues: (IV.xii.1)

> O what an endlesse worke have I in hand,
>> To count the seas abundant progeny,
>> Whose fruitfull seede farre passeth those in land,
>> And also those which wonne in th'azure sky?
>> For much more eath to tell the starres on hy,
>> Albe they endlesse seeme in estimation,
>> Then to recount the Seas posterity:
>> So fertile be the flouds in generation,
> So huge their numbers, and so numberlesse their nation.

Everywhere the poem displays his ceaseless curiosity about words: their etymology, history, and imagery; their clash of literal and metaphorical meanings; and the rivalry of meanings which expresses their life. Puns, quibbles, and riddles may emerge anywhere. When words fail him, he invents new ones or revives obsolete senses. He labours ceaselessly to make each word contain and express its nature.

Etymology is one major poetic device by which Spenser forces a word to express its true meanings. The etymology of his names has been noted in a number of recent studies, and in unpublished doctoral dissertations by Martha Craig, Alice Blitch, and, thoroughly, by J. Belson.[5] These studies show how a character's name reveals his nature and function in the allegory. For example, the etymology of the Red Cross Knight's name has been known since 1758 when Upton noted that Voragine's *Golden Legend* was Spenser's source for the life of St George. According to the *Legend*, 'George is sayd of geos / whiche is as moche to saye as erthe and orge / that is tilyenge / so george is to saye as tilyenge the erthe / that is his flesshe ... Or George may be sayd of gera: that is holy / and of gyon that is a wrasteler / that is an holy wrasteler. For he wrasteled with the dragon.'[6] Spenser frames the Knight's character and actions through an awareness of such etymologies. He is found in a ploughman's furrow and raised in ploughman's state by which he gains his name (x.66); he is associated with Orgoglio, his fallen form, by a shared etymology – Ge-*orgos*, *Orgo*-glio (the latter also linked with a furrow, viii.8); and he is associated with Guyon, his natural form, as both are wrestlers.[7] Like Adam, he is named after the earth of which he is made: hence Contemplation names him simply 'thou man of earth' (x.52).

Witty playing upon the complex etymology of names obsessed Spenser so entirely throughout the poem that one may suspect an oblique allusion to the Queen's name in the closing lines where he prays for the time when 'all shall rest eternally / With Him that is the God of Sabbaoth hight: / O that great Sabbaoth God, graunt me that Sabaoths sight.' Since Spenser would know that 'Sabbath' signifies 'rest,' his final prayer at the end of his six days of labour is for sight of that day of rest: that great Sabbath and eternal rest. Since he would know also that Elizabeth signifies 'Peace of the Lord, or quiet rest of the Lord,'[8] his final prayer as an exile in war-ravaged Ireland is for sight of the Queen and the rest which she signifies. It is also Arthur's prayer for the sight of his Faery Queen. Such speculation suggests that if one fully understood the poem's names, one would fully understand its allegory.

Interest in etymology leads Spenser to employ etymological spelling and the etymological epithet. Hence Orgoglio is called a 'Geant' (i.vii.8) because he is the son of Gea, the earth; Duessa's breath 'abhominably smeld' (i.viii.47) because she is *ab homine*, from man and hence beastly; Phaedria's lake is named the *'Ydle lake'* in the lines cited above because the gnostic Y describes the paths of virtue and vice which Phaedria places before man; and the feminine in opposition to the masculine is spelled 'fœminine' at ii.ix.22 because it is the 'foe to man.' Where spelling does not work, Spenser uses an epithet. As a general rule an epithet defines; rarely is it simply descriptive. In the catalogue of beasts tamed by Satyrane each is cited in its characteristic strength in order to show his superior power: (i.vi.26)

> The spotted Panther, and the tusked Bore,
> The Pardale swift, and the Tigre cruell;
> The Antelope, and Wolfe both fierce and fell.

An exception to the rule would seem to be the 'spotted Panther' until one learns that the beast was thought to attract its prey by its spotted hide. The best known example of Spenser's use of the characterizing epithet is found in the catalogue of the rivers at iv.xi where he labours to give the rivers 'their righte names.'[9] More representative of his use is his account of 'The Rock of vile *Reproch'* which Guyon encounters on his voyage to Acrasia's Bower. Since the Rock wrecks those of 'lost credite and consumed thrift,' it is a 'daungerous' place in the obsolete sense of 'to be in danger': to be in debt (OED 1). It is attended by 'yelling Meawes, with Seagulles hoarse and bace, / And Cormoyrants, with birds of ravenous race' (ii.xii.8). 'Meawes' attend because the word signifies 'prison,' and they are 'yelling' because the echoic verb 'mew,' which we apply to cats, was applied to seabirds in the sixteenth century. Gulls are present because the word signifies 'trickery,' and hence they are called 'bace.' 'Cormoyrant' was a term applied to usurers; and being a sea-raven, it is called 'ravenous.' These birds watch 'on that wastfull clift' because the rock is a fitting punishment for the wasteful. Often the etymological epithet expands into a brief allegory. The jealous Malbecco feeds on dread 'That doth with curelesse care consume the hart' (iii.x.59). 'Care' is 'curelesse' because the word comes from Latin *cura*, care; it consumes the heart because of its received etymology: *cura quod cor edat*, which Spenser's phrase directly translates.

Etymology and associated word-play may initiate the larger action of a canto as it does in the poem's opening episode. The Knight's journey through the Wandering Wood to Error's den becomes one extended pun as complex in its way as a chapter of *Finnegans Wake*. I shall follow only a few threads through that labyrinth. The 'harbour' or place of retreat which the Knight and Una seek to protect them from the storm becomes an arbour or shady retreat. At first they cannot see the wood for the trees; but once they do, 'in diverse doubt they been.' 'Doubt,' with the added sense 'fear,' is 'diverse' in a sense peculiar to Spenser: it is distracting, from the etymological sense 'turned different ways.' At the centre of the Wandering Wood is Error's den whose hidden danger 'breedes dreadfull doubts.' It follows, then, that the Knight sees Error with her brood. Her half-woman shape embodies the pleasures of the Wandering Wood; her tail, the labyrinth which entangles the Knight in doubt; and its mortal sting, death which comes at the end. When she sees him, she rushes from her den, 'hurling her hideous taile / About her cursed head, whose folds displaid / Were stretcht now forth at length without entraile.' 'Hurling,' which combines 'hurtling' and 'whirling' later expresses the violent motion of Lucifera (iv.16), Orgoglio (viii.17), and the Dragon (xi.23). 'Entraile' combines the noun which signifies 'intestines' and the verb 'entwine': hence it combines the entwined and entwining paths of the labyrinth and the beast's entrails which now surround the Knight. When she winds her 'huge traine' or tail about him, the poet adds in the next line 'God helpe the man so wrapt in *Errours* endlesse traine.' The duplicated rhyme, 'traine,' signifies treachery or deceit, thus linking the literal and allegorical senses of the monster's tail with the Wandering Wood. Una is sad to see his 'sore constraint,' i.e., his fettered state, the term being used in the etymological sense of the Latin *constringere*, 'to draw tight.' The Knight endures 'in great perplexitie,' referring to his mental bewilderment, to his physical distress (now an obsolete sense), and literally to his entangled state (from the Latin *perplex*). When he strangles the monster, she spews her filthy 'parbreake' upon him: this term for vomit is used here in its etymological sense, 'breaking out,' in order to indicate the monster's violence which is first shown when she 'upstart[s]' upon seeing the Knight.

After the Knight defeats Error, he wrestles with Archimago's 'diverse dreame' (44): again 'diverse' suggests its etymological sense, 'turning different ways' because Archimago endeavours to separate him from Una. Hence it adds the sense of the Italian *diverso*, 'wicked, perverse.' In response to the dream, for fear 'of doing aught amis, / He started up' (49), which is the characteristic action of Error. Afterwards he is left 'musing' (55), i.e., wandering in a mental maze. In the final stage of his deception, when his sleep is broken by Archimago's news of the false pair, 'All in amaze he suddenly up start' (ii.5): clearly he is now Error's victim.

The Knight flees from Una leaving them both 'divided into double parts' (ii.9). Here 'double' carries an added sense, 'divided': he is divided *from* himself so that now he is first named when the false St George appears as the disguised Archimago, and divided *in* himself so that he meets aspects of himself in Sansfoy, Sansjoy, and finally Orgoglio. Una cannot be divided in herself, being one; yet she is divided from herself so that she is first named when the false Una appears (i.45) and again (ii.9) before the entrance of her double, Duessa. She is 'from her knight divorced in despaire / And her due loves deriv'd to that vile witches share' (iii.2): here 'divorced' is used in the explicit sense, 'dissolving the marriage contract,' for her love is diverted or drawn away (from *divertium*, the Latin root of 'divorce') when he pledges himself to Duessa 'in safe assauraunce' (ii.27). Accordingly, when Una meets him again, she says: 'welcome now my Lord, in wele or woe' (viii.43), by these words renewing their marriage vow. Here I leave this labyrinth of etymologies: I tire, as you must, though Spenser never does.

I shall leave the subject, too, after illustrating how etymology may outline the scope of an action that extends through several books. In his story of Florimell's flight Spenser pauses at mid-point. Already he has subjected her to the terrors of the land and is about to subject her to the terrors of the sea until she remains imprisoned 'under a mightie rocke' (iii.viii.37) because of her constant love for Marinell. The moment is crucial to her story: up to this point her flight has not been unusual: it imitates the flight of heroines of romance, such as Angelica's at the opening of *Orlando Furioso*. From this point, however, her flight involves metamorphosis and 'death': it imitates that of Britomartis of classical legend, to whom, as Britomart, Florimell now acts as surrogate. The poet laments: (iii.viii.1)

> So oft as I this history record,
>   My hart doth melt with meere compassion,
>   To thinke, how causelesse of her owne accord
>   This gentle Damzell, whom I write upon,
>   Should plonged be in such affliction,
>   Without all hope of comfort or reliefe,
>   That sure I weene, the hardest hart of stone,
>   Would hardly find to aggravate her griefe;
> For misery craves rather mercie, then repriefe.

In anticipation of the action 'affliction' is used in its etymological sense, 'thrown down': literally, she is to be thrown down to the bottom of the sea. 'Aggravate' is also used in its etymological sense, 'weigh down,' 'put weight on': literally she is to be held under a rock. I note in passing as examples of word-play that 'find' implies 'find the means to' but also 'devise, invent': despite his pity, the poet intends to aggravate Florimell's grief. Also 'the hardest hart of stone' alludes to Marinell's 'stony heart' (iv.xii.13) for his rejection of love – taught him by his mother therefore in a 'rocky cave' (iii.iv.20) – brings Florimell's imprisonment in walls of stone.

Spenser's delight in etymology is one part of his enormous pleasure, which he expects his readers to share, in all kinds of witty word-play. Puns spring up everywhere, most frequently in erotic episodes, but they may be found at any place where the pressure of meaning overloads a word's normal range of significance. They range from the simplest play upon double senses – 'dismall day,' for example, is hardly more than a schoolboy's howler on its root, *dies mali* – to the most serious conjunction of different senses. Dame Caelia greets Una with an apostrophe to the 'happie earth, / Whereon thy innocent feet doe ever tread, ... Yet ceasest not thy wearie soles to lead' (i.x.9): 'soles' refers to men's souls as pilgrims which are in the keeping of the Church. Before the Knight encounters the Dragon, Una warns him: 'henceforth be at your keeping well' (i.xi.2): she means that if he wishes to triumph, he must be on his guard and also at the Well of Life which will keep him well. At the outset of the battle the Dragon 'made wide shadow under his huge wast' (i.xi.8): 'wast' refers both to his body and to the vast expanse (Latin *vastus*) of land reduced to a waste by this shadow of death. During the battle his flames 'swinged' the Knight's beard – the term means both scorched and whipped – so that 'through his armour all his bodie seard / That he could not endure so cruell cace' (i.xi.26). 'Seard' means literally 'burned by hot iron'; 'cace' refers both to the Knight's plight and to the armour which burns him. Such word-play points to the central paradox that the armour which defends him and later slays the Dragon now causes him to fall, but to fall so that he may arise renewed. This paradox is enforced by the jingle of echoing rhymes in the next stanza: 'fyrie steele now burnt, that earst him arm'd, / That erst him goodly arm'd, now most of all him harm'd.'

Through extended use a pun may become part of the language of allegory. For example, 'incontinent' signifies both 'intemperate' in the literal sense of not restraining oneself and 'immediately.' Throughout the poem both senses are usually present. In Book i Arthur gives the Red Cross Knight a 'few drops of liquor pure, ... That any wound could heale incontinent' (ix.19). In Book ii it is said that if man's body is not kept in sober government 'it growes a Monster, and incontinent / Doth loose his dignitie and native grace' (ix.1). In Book iii Britomart laments by the seashore at the beginning of her quest: she compares her state to a storm-tossed ship and appeals for 'some gentle gale of ease' from the God of Winds 'that raignest in the seas, / That raignest also in the Continent' (iv.10), referring to those who are ruled by Love and those who are continent. As she soon discovers, the land is ruled by the continent Marinell. When he is wounded by her, his mother comes from the ocean and 'threw her selfe downe on the Continent' (iv.30). Here the pun clarifies the nature of Marinell, a creature of the land and sea, and suggests why his marriage to Florimell, a creature of the land held by the sea, should resolve the action of Books III and IV. When this same word-play occurs in the following canto, it hardly constitutes a pun: the separate meanings have merged. Timias slays the lustful Foster 'Right as he entring was into the flood': and fittingly 'The carkas with the streame was carried downe, / But th'head fell backeward on the Continent' (v.25).

The simplest kind of word-play is repetition of a word. When the 'dead' Guyon is defended by Arthur, his body is called a 'carcass' four times within a few stanzas. Such repetition enforces the literal sense of that word, 'fallen flesh,' and clarifies Arthur's redemption of Guyon. In this same episode Guyon's enemies are repeatedly called 'pagans' or 'paynim' brothers, terms not used since Book I where they describe the Red Cross Knight's enemies. (With one exception their use is restricted to this episode.) Such repeated use suggests that now God has directly intervened on behalf of Guyon, Guyon's enemies have become his. When a word is repeated in different contexts, it may accumulate meanings so that it becomes a centre of our understanding.[10] One example is the word-play upon 'heart' in the Despair episode. Earlier Duessa brandished her charmed cup from which 'Death and despeyre did many thereof sup, ... Th'eternall bale of heavie wounded harts' (I.viii.14). Though Death is defeated when the Knight is rescued from the dungeon, Despair remains. When he confronts Trevisan who flees Despair, he seeks by 'bold hartie speach' to embolden his 'bloud-frosen hart' (ix.25). He cannot do so because he and his companion were overcome by Despair when he 'felt our feeble harts / Embost with bale' (29). This pun on 'heart' – a hunted hart is 'embost' when it foams with fatigue – introduces elaborate play upon the word when the Knight himself confronts Despair. At the end Despair's speech pierces his heart until Una's speech persuades him not to let 'vaine words bewitch [his] manly hart' (53). Since the poem is an elaborately constructed allegory, any word in it may become a latent pun.

Word-play may be displayed through ambiguous syntax.[11]

Spenser commonly employs the floating adjective or adverb. When Guyon confronts Mammon, he (ii.vii.6)

> lightly to him leaping, stayd
> His hand, that trembled, as one terrifyde;
> And though him selfe were at the sight dismayd,
> Yet him perforce restraynd, and to him doubtfull sayd.

'To him doubtfull': i.e., to the fearful Mammon. Yet the term applies equally to Guyon: he is doubtful about Mammon's identity and fearful – as 'dismayd' suggests – of the temptation that confronts him. Pronouns may be used ambiguously, as one would expect in an allegory where characters are states, and action consists of conflict between projections of a character or aspects of his state. When Britomart holds her sword over Busyrane to force him to recite the charms that may free Amoret, (iii.xii.37)

> Anon she gan perceive the house to quake,
> And all the dores to rattle round about;
> Yet all that did not her dismaied make,
> Nor slacke her threatfull hand for daungers dout,
> But still with stedfast eye and courage stout
> Abode, to weet what end would come of all.
> At last that mightie chaine, which round about
> Her tender waste was wound, adowne gan fall,
> And that great brasen pillour broke in peeces small.

If we were reading a novel, we would understand immediately that 'her tender waste' refers to Amoret. Since we are reading an allegory, the reference remains ambiguous in order to avoid confusion. A similar, brilliant example of ambiguity is found in the concluding words of Book i canto xi. After the Knight has slain the Dragon, Una approaches to praise him:

> Then God she praysd, and thankt her faithfull knight,
> That had atchiev'd so great a conquest by his might.

'By his might' refers both to God and to the Knight; in so doing it resolves the action of the episode and the book. Since God's grace is fully manifest in man's might, the Knight is seen in the lineaments of Christ, the Dragon-killer.

117 Spenser, 'well of English undefyld'

In considering Spenser's art of language I have been singling out examples that are special, though numerous. At any point in the poem, however, a reader is impressed by Spenser's witty play upon the meanings of words and their emotive and imaginative impact. Typically Spenserian is the vaguely suggestive word: 'dreriment,' mentioned earlier, is a representative example. After the Red Cross Knight hears Fradubio's story, he is left 'Full of sad feare and ghastly dreriment' (i.ii.44). Although the word has not occurred before in the poem, and its formation – adding '-ment' to an adjective – is unusual, its general sense causes no problem. It is glossed 'dreery and heavy cheere' by E.K. when it occurs in *The Shepheardes Calender* November eclogue. 'Ghastly dreriment' functions chiefly to give weight to the simple phrase 'sad feare.' While 'ghastly' suggests explicitly the terror evoked by the sight of a ghost, here Fradubio's, 'dreriment' remains purposely vague. By remaining vague, it expresses the ominous, nightmarish, and unrealized 'sad feare' from which the Knight suffers. His inner fear takes shape in outer action only later when he encounters the person of Sansjoy. 'Dreriment' belongs to a word-play extended throughout Book i: the Knight enters upon his quest 'too solemne sad' (i.2); during it he calls upon death on four occasions; and only by passing through the house of Penaunce does he learn 'himselfe to chearish' (x.29).

Another typically Spenserian word is 'griesly.' When we read that Phaedria's boat drives through 'the slouthfull wave of that great griesly lake' (ii.vi.18), we understand that word at first as though it meant 'horrible.' Spenser allies the word to 'griesy' and by extended use of both seeks their latent, active sense, 'producing horror' (from Old French *gris*). In the episode above we learn later that (vi.46)

> The waves thereof so slow and sluggish were,
> Engrost with mud, which did them foul agrise,
> That every weightie thing they did upbeare.

When these waters, acting contrary to their nature, fail to quench Pyrochles' inner flames, instead rendering him more foul, it becomes clear why they arouse horror, why they are called 'griesly.'

Throughout his poem Spenser defines the meanings of his words by careful, precise use and by parallel but significantly different use in a variety of contexts. He may begin by exploiting the multiple meanings of words he inherits. Adonis is slain by the boar that 'with his cruell tuske him deadly cloyd' (iii.vi.48). Here 'cloyd' signifies 'pierced, gored' (cf. OED $v.^1$3); also, since the boar signifies lust and his wound concupiscence, the term includes its modern sense, 'the surfeiting of desire.' When Cymochles lies in the Bower surrounded by naked maidens, 'some bathed kisses, and did soft embrew / The sugred licour through his melting lips' (ii.v.33). The OED cites the use of 'embrew' as unique and accepts Johnson's definition, 'pour, emit moisture.' From the etymological sense the meaning is 'cause to drink'; however, the entire range of sixteenth-century meanings is implied: steep, thrust, stain, and infect. Betrayed by Duessa, the Red Cross Knight is called 'dissolute' (i.vii.51). The term means debauched, enfeebled, relaxed, and careless. Also it implies 'dissolved' (OED 1), from the Latin *dissolutus,* loose: the Knight was betrayed when he lay 'pourd out in loosnesse on the grassy grownd' (vii.7). Yet further, one must allow that here, as always, Spenser says what he means and means what he says: the Knight is 'dissolute' in the precise sense of being dissolved: by drinking from the fountain, his 'chearefull bloud in faintnesse chill did melt' (vii.6), that is, his blood is corrupted into the polluted water which he drinks.

When inherited words could not be adapted to serve his needs, Spenser invented new ones. Fully representative of his usual practice are his coinages[12] in the stanzas which describe Arthur's battle with Cymochles. Arthur thrusts his spear 'That through his thigh the mortall steele did gryde' (ii.viii.36). Obviously Spenser delights in the antique word 'gryde' (which E.K. defines as 'pierce' in his gloss to the February eclogue) because it conveys the grating sound of the weapon as it tears through flesh with rasping pain. When the spear breaks, the blood flows 'That underneath his feet soone made a purple plesh': here alliteration conveys the onomatopoeic origin of 'plesh.' Arthur strikes twice at Cymochles, 'that twise him forst his foot revoke' (39): 'revoke' signifies 'withdraw,' cited by OED as a unique usage.

The term may be modelled upon the Latin phrase, *revocare pedem*, though the general sense of the word, 'to call back,' sufficiently accounts for its use. In his anger Arthur fights like a lion that 'wexeth wood and yond' (40): 'yond' has been taken as Spenser's misunderstanding of Chaucer's 'egre as is a tygre yond in Inde,' but Martha Craig suggests more correctly that 'wood and yond' implies 'madness and going beyond madness.' Arthur fights as a savage bull 'When rancour doth with rage him once engore' (42). 'Engore' implies the effect of his being goaded: rancour and rage cause him to engore his enemy. He fights 'renfierst with wrath' (45): here 'renfierst' is a portmanteau word that means both 're-enforced' and 'rendered more fierce.'

More interesting are those many moments in the poem when the sheer pressure of the allegory forces Spenser to fashion a new word. I offer two examples, only one of which I believe I understand. When Una's parents may at last leave their besieged castle, they go to the field 'where that champion stout / After his foes defeasance did remaine' (i.xii.12). The sense of 'defeasance,' defeat, is attributed to Spenser by OED; it is used only here. Yet Spenser does not use the word 'defeat' but fashions a new sense by adapting an earlier legal sense, from the French 'defesaunce,' which means 'to render a claim null and void.' Spenser uses 'defeasance,' then, to note that the Dragon usurped Adam's kingdom: by his defeat, his claim to the land now ends. Una's parents ruled 'from East to Westerne shore' (i.i.5) until they were expelled by the Dragon, and in their place Duessa's parents now rule only 'the wide West' (ii.22). The prior claim of Una's parents to Eden has extended political, religious, and ecclesiastical significance which 'defeasance' is coined to clarify.

My second example is more interesting though puzzling. After the Red Cross Knight had been rudely attacked by Guyon, he asks him courteously: (ii.i.29)

> Now mote I weet,
> Sir *Guyon*, why with so fierce saliaunce,
> And fell intent ye did at earst me meet;
> For sith I know your goodly governaunce.

Apparently from the context 'saliaunce' means 'assault, onslaught.' Evidently it is coined from *saliaunt, salire,* to leap, by way of the heraldic term 'salient,' which is the posture of leaping. I suspect that the term holds heraldic significance which I fail to understand. This much does seem clear: the term stresses Guyon's hasty violence in attacking the Red Cross Knight without a formal challenge. Later Pyrochles attacks Arthur in the same manner: he gains the reproof and punishment which Guyon here for his intent deserves, and vicariously receives (II.viii.31). In this connection it would seem relevant that 'sallied,' that is, 'leapt,' is used twice in the poem: it describes Guyon's leaping from Phaedria's boat to continue his journey to the Bower (vi.38) and his leaping from the mariner's boat to enter Acrasia's realm (xii.38).

Through his art of language Spenser seeks to purify words by restoring them to their true, original meanings. When Adam fell, he lost that natural language in which words contain and reveal the realities they name.[18] Though corrupt, languages remain divinely given and the poet's burden is to purify the language of his own tribe. Words have been 'wrested from their true calling': the poet attempts to wrest them back. Spenser 'writ no language,' as Jonson noted: that is, he avoids a fallen language which would only confirm man in his state of bondage. By his language of allegory he recreates that natural language in which the word and its reality again merge. Like Adam, he gives names to his creatures which express their natures. He shares Bacon's distrust of language and even his scorn for those who care more for words than matter. His word-play is not an idle game but a sustained and serious effort to plant words as seeds in the reader's imagination. In Jonson's phrase he 'makes their minds like the thing he writes.'[14] He shares Bacon's faith that the true end of knowledge is 'a restitution and reinvesting (in great part) of man to the sovereignty and power (for whensoever he shall be able to call the creatures by their true names he shall again command them) which he had in his first state of creation.'[15] Although his poem remains largely unfinished, he has restored at least those words which are capable of fashioning his reader in virtuous and gentle discipline.

NOTES

1 *Critical Approaches to Six Major English Works,* ed. R.M. Lumiansky and Herschel Baker (Philadelphia, 1968), pp. 160–1.

2 E.K.'s praise of *The Shepheardes Calender* in his dedicatory epistle.

3 Constantine Fitzgibbon, *The Life of Dylan Thomas* (Boston: Atlantic-Little, Brown, 1965), p. 371.

4 *An Apology for Poetry,* ed. G. Shepherd (London, 1965), p. 140.

5 Martha Craig, 'Language and Concept in *The Faerie Queene*,' doctoral dissertation, Yale University, 1959, and see her 'The Secret Wit of Spenser's Language,' in *Elizabethan Poetry,* ed. Paul J. Alpers (New York, 1967), pp. 447–72; Alice Blitch, 'Etymon and Image in *The Faerie Queene,*' doctoral dissertation, Michigan State University, 1965; J. Belson, 'The Names in *The Faerie Queene,*' doctoral dissertation, Columbia University, 1964. See also the important general article, K.K. Ruthven, 'The Poet as Etymologist,' *Critical Quarterly* 11 (1969), 9–37.

6 *The lyfe of Saynt George,* reprinted from Caxton's translation of *The Golden Legend* (Wynkyn de Worde, 1512), in Alexander Barclay's *The Life of St. George,* EETS o.s. 230 (London, 1955), p. 112. See William Nelson, *The Poetry of Edmund Spenser* (New York, 1963), p. 151.

7 See Susan Snyder, 'Guyon the Wrestler,' *Renaissance News* 14 (1961), 249–52.

8 William Camden, *Remains concerning Britain* (first printed 1605; London, 1870), p. 102.

9 From Spenser's account of his *Epithalamion Thamesis,* in 'Three proper wittie familiar letters,' in *Poetical Works,* ed. J.C. Smith and E. de Selincourt (Oxford, 1912), p. 612.

10 A.W. Satterthwaite observes that 'Spenser's words are heavily fraught with the meanings they acquire through their repeated use in certain contexts in his whole work. They become as "loaded" as any words a poet ever used' (*Spenser, Ronsard, and Du Bellay: A Renaissance Comparison,* Princeton, 1960, p. 154, n. 21). Cf. Kathleen Williams's penetrating comment on the phrase 'they that love do live' (III.iv.37): 'The words themselves – life, death, love – are flat through long use and misuse, and any writer must recharge them if we are to be convinced that he is dealing not in paltry effects of verbal jugglery but in a felt paradox. Spenser does recharge them; they are the explosive point of an accumulated force coming from the finely structured narrative and its images' (*Spenser's 'Faerie Queene': The World of Glass,* London, 1966, p. 142).

11 Paul J. Alpers has some illuminating comments on this topic in *The Poetry of 'The Faerie Queene'* (Princeton, 1967), pp. 77–95.

12 I use the term loosely: properly speaking, coinages are only those words coined by Spenser which are unhistorical in development or uncertain in origin. See Bruce R. McElderry, 'Archaism and Innovation in Spenser's Poetic Diction,' *PMLA* 47 (1932), 161.

13 See Arnold Williams, *The Common Expositor* (Chapel Hill, 1948), pp. 228–32.

14 *Discoveries*, in *Works*, ed. C.H. Herford and P. and E. Simpson (Oxford, 1947), VIII, 588.

15 *Valerius Terminus*, in *Philosophical Works*, ed. J.M. Robertson (London, 1905), p. 188. On the Elizabethan attitude towards language see M.M. Mahood, *Shakespeare's Wordplay* (London, 1957), pp. 169–75. See Christopher Ricks's account of Milton's effort to 're-create something of the pre-lapsarian state of language' (*Milton's Grand Style*, Oxford, 1963, pp. 110ff.).

123 Spenser, 'well of English undefyld'

Spenser's *Amoretti* and the English sonnet tradition

G.K. HUNTER

Spenser's *Amoretti* were published by William Ponsonby in 1595: *Amoretti and Epithalamion. Written not long since by Edmund Spenser.* The publishing of a set of sonnets and an epithalamion together may be the result of the accident that these poems all came into Ponsonby's hands at the same time; and this supposition must be strengthened by the presence of a set of anacreontic verses at the end of the sonnets and before the separate title-page of the *Epithalamion.* So far as I know, no one has ever made satisfactory sense of the placing of these anacreontics. Louis Martz remarked in his 1961 English Institute Essay: 'I have only one solution to offer for the intervening anacreontics: ignore them.'[1] I am forced to concur with this; and forced therefore to accept also that the haphazard addition of the anacreontic verses casts doubt on any system of order one imagines for the book as a whole. I ought to add that the apparently casual repetition of sonnet 35 as sonnet 83 (I reject Martz's melioration) points in the same direction.[2]

On the other hand, no other collection of sonnets ends in an epithalamion, so far as I know. It follows that the idea of combining the two genres cannot have occurred to Ponsonby as a natural relationship of parts. And the *Amoretti* themselves give *some* indication that they are arranged as the history of a courtship leading up to marriage, or the expectation of marriage – and this again is not the natural or inevitable end to a sonnet sequence. As early as sonnet 6 the lady is being urged, not to yield to her lover in the common mode, but to

think ...
To knit the knot that ever shall remain.

This must refer to the marriage-knot. But such a sonnet might be regarded as a 'sport' in the sequence, were it not that after sonnet 62 the prevailing tone of the sequence changes. In 63 the lover 'at length descrie[s] the happy shore.' In 64 he 'com[es] to kiss her lips (such grace I found).' In 65 he argues against the loss of liberty in a tied relationship – presumably marriage. In 67 he captures the deer or hart that had earlier escaped from him. Sonnet 68 ('Most glorious lord of life ...') implies a relationship which is emotionally fast and lacks only the sacramental seal of holy matrimony: 'grant that we ... Being ... washed from sin, / May live forever in felicity.' Sonnet 69 speaks with assurance of

> The happy purchase of my glorious spoil
> Gotten at last with labour and long toil,

as if the reader was intended at this point to recognize what 'labour and long toil' refer to, and to document the details from the many images of frustration and cruelty that appear earlier in the sequence. And so on. There is more evidence of a general shift of tone at the end of the sequence than most readers have patience to bear. Of course I am not implying that every sonnet has its correct place in the jigsaw, the complete consort dancing together

> The association of man and woman
> In dauncinge, signifying matrimonie ...

I do not believe that any of the major English collections of sonnets ever existed in a simple sequential order in which every element is contained or explained; or indeed that we are able to rearrange any of the sequences into an original or true order, with every hair restored to its proper place. I assume that a high proportion of casual elements is of the essence, and that it is a vanity of human pride to try to make them disappear. So I do not allege that what I have called a change of tone after sonnet 62 (or so) affects every sonnet on either side of this divide. I only propose that it is marked enough to make the relation between the sequence and the *Epithalamion* seem (arguably) intended by Spenser.

If the *Amoretti* gives in this limited sense 'the history of a courtship' leading up to matrimony, and if the *Epithalamion* celebrates the actual wedding, then we have the image of an emotional development portrayed throughout its length in poetry. It becomes proper then to compare the different parts of the process one with another, and in particular to compare the sonnets with the *Epithalamion*. And here I intend to offer a simple but I hope not abhorrent value-judgment. The *Epithalamion* I take to be the greatest of Spenser's minor poems: it is sonorous, rich, powerful, moving, coherent, and no doubt many other good things. On the other hand, the *Amoretti* range from the mediocre to the good, but do not achieve anything like the sustained excellence of the *Epithalamion*. My paper is concerned with the question why this should be so.

One possible answer to the question invokes the casual element I have myself upheld. One poem is better than another just because it happens to be so, or because the poet had eaten something that agreed with him, or chanced on some other source of inspiration. Some of this is no doubt true of the *Amoretti*; but it could hardly be true of all 89 sonnets. Or the *Amoretti* may have been written at a much earlier stage in Spenser's development. One could multiply imponderables indefinitely; but I wish to speak of the inferiority of the *Amoretti* and the superiority of the *Epithalamion* in more basic terms. I believe that their relative merits could have been forecast from a proper reading of *The Faerie Queene*; for the mode of one reflects a habitual weakness in Spenser's verse, while the mode of the other reflects a habitual strength. One can say this the opposite way round, and at some points it is more convenient to do so: it is a worthwhile exercise to look at the difference between the *Amoretti* and the *Epithalamion* because of what it tells us about the strengths and weaknesses of Spenser's verse everywhere.

The excellence of the *Epithalamion* derives in part from Spenser's capacity in this poem to use the facts of real life as a framework upon which, by mythological and biblical parallels, he throws what a later age was to call the colouring of imagination – the sense of a sacramental occasion, representative of human destiny, at once this wedding and all weddings, and not only all weddings but all sanctifications of fertility. St Barnabas's Day is not only a date for the wedding but also the summer solstice, the centre of the year's fertility and the hallowing of this in the church calendar. The pattern or progress of the poem is the progress of a real day; but the order of a real day is only a transparency through which we see a further and higher order, which real days represent only as an outer integument.

A marriage day has a built-in structure; already in real life it is the object of sanctifying imagination and ritual. A courtship is, however, much less obvious in its possession of such a structure – especially if it is conceived as a personal and not simply a social sequence of events. It is correspondingly more difficult to sacramentalize. In *The Faerie Queene* the only courtship which is of any length is that of Scudamour and Amoret in Book IV canto x – for the seduction of Hellenore by Paridell I take to be anti-sacramental – and it is interesting to note that Scudamour's wooing is conducted entirely in allegorical terms. His conquest of his namesake the shield of love (or *escu d'Amour*), his passing through Doubt, Delay, Daunger, his discovery of Venus and her handmaids, Modesty, Silence, Courtesy, Obedience, and Womanhood – all this corresponds to elements in the *Amoretti*; but there is very little correspondence in the imagery or the structure of the situations. It is as if the allegorical imagination which supports Book IV canto x was of no use to Spenser when he was writing the *Amoretti*. And it is easy to see why. The *Amoretti*, if they were to lead up to the *Epithalamion*, would have to refer to a personal situation which, however ritualized, could not be expressed by the generalizing methods of *The Faerie Queene*. There was, moreover, a literary tradition concerned with a personal approach to courtship already available – the English sonnet sequence written in imitation of Petrarch, which, as J.W. Lever has remarked, 'aimed above all else at the voicing of personal perceptions.'[3] I say the English sonnet sequence because I believe that the case of Petrarch himself may be rather different. In any case Petrarch himself is hardly necessary for the argument; the English sonnet was well established before Spenser wrote the *Amoretti*; the centrality of the developing relationship between a highly individualized man and his imagination of his lady was already clear. This was especially true in the sequence that must have loomed largest in Spenser's eye – Sidney's *Astrophil and Stella*. Sidney had been Spenser's patron, and was the ideal figure to whom he had been making obeisance since youth. But *Astrophil and Stella* may have had a further and more precise importance for the *Amoretti*: it may have provided the sequence with what looked like an exact model. Spenser and Bryskett seem to have believed that Lady Sidney (Frances Walsingham) was Stella.[4] Looked at from this point of view, *Astrophil and Stella* seems to trace a courtship leading up to marriage, even though it ends with themes of separation and mourning.

It is mere hypothesis that Spenser saw the *Astrophil and Stella* as a model for a sonnet sequence that could lead up to the *Epithalamion*; but, if it is true, then Spenser must have failed to notice the rather basic differences that separated Sidney's poetic genius from his own. For these were bound to make his own sonnet sequence quite unlike Sidney's. *Astrophil and Stella* is really a series of exercises in self-definition: Stella's role is to act as a mirror reflecting Astrophil's emotional states. The poems describe what it is like to go on being aware of oneself as a man and yet to be in love. Spenser's sequence is far more concerned with the relationship and far less with the individual. The lover's 'I' or ego is often completely ignored and even where mentioned is usually absorbed into a pattern which aborts self-definition. Take sonnet 16:

> One day as I unwarily did gaze
> On those fair eyes, my love's immortal light,
> The whiles my 'stonished heart stood in amaze
> Through sweet illusion of her look's delight,
> I mote perceive how in her glancing sight
> Legions of loves with little wings did fly,
> Darting their deadly arrows fiery-bright
> At every rash beholder passing by.
> One of those archers closely I did spy
> Aiming his arrow at my very heart,
> When suddenly with twinkle of her eye
> The damsel broke his misintended dart.
> Had she not so done, sure I had been slain;
> Yet as it was, I hardly scaped with pain.

The single long sentence with its suspended syntax which makes up the first eight lines reflects a unified and static situation. There is no room for the contrasts or the sharp turns of direction by which the ego is given dramatic focus. The contrast between death and pain with which the final couplet tries to define an action in the poem is obviously insufficient to create any retrospective tension. The heavy drone of the rhythm and the archaic calm of the conventionalized vocabulary repress the tensions of individualism. The adjective-noun groupings – fair eyes, immortal light, 'stonished heart, sweet illusion, glancing sight, little wings, deadly arrows, etc. – clearly do not aim at producing any shock of recognition, or indeed any other shock. The Spenserian interlinking of the rhyme-schemes of the stanzas encourages the same calming effect on a larger scale. If we compare with this sonnet some lines from Sidney's ninety-second sonnet –

When I demand of Phoenix Stella's state,
You say, forsooth, you left her well of late.
O God, think you that satisfies my care?
I would know whether she did sit or walk,
How clothed, how waited on, sighed she or smiled –

we notice in contrast the rapid shift from implied third to second, and then to first person, the vigorous counterpointing of speech against verse; these remind us of a Shakespeare play – say *Antony and Cleopatra* – rather than the *Amoretti*.

In Sidney's sequence the ego of the lover is defined by dramatic contrasts, such as that between his inner life and the external world in which he continues to exist. In sonnet 51 and sonnet 30 –

Whether the Turkish new moon minded be
To fill his horns this year on Christian coast –

a tedious interlocutor asks questions about politics while the lover thinks only about Stella. In sonnet 41 he is praised for his horsemanship and other gifts; only *he* knows that the inspiration for all these comes from Stella. In sonnet 53 he forgets that he should be jousting and stands staring at Stella instead, while she blushes for the absurdity of his appearance. In other sonnets the ego is defined by the distinction between 'Aganippe's well' or other 'inventions fine' which 'dainty wits' depend on – between the whole vocabulary of the Petrarchans – and the 'true' or 'plain' inner world of this individual. But not only do Sidney's sonnets differ from Spenser's by being built up on effects of contrast; more differentiating still is the point that the contrast is often ironic or even comic. The author invites the reader to share a sense of comic disproportion between inner and outer. The lover is presented by the author with a certain *sprezzatura*; the author looks down with detachment on the situations and emotions of the lover, even on the rhetoric the lover uses to express himself.

When the inner world of the lover and the outer reality of the author appear together in the *Amoretti* (as in sonnet 33) the effect is quite different. In sonnet 33 Spenser is complaining to Lodowick that he feels guilty about not finishing *The Faerie Queene*, but cannot do so while his mind 'is tost with troublous fit':

> Great wrong I do, I can it not deny,
> To that most sacred Empress, my dear dread,
> Not finishing her Queene of Faerie
> That mote enlarge her living praises dead.
> But, Lod'wick, this of grace to me aread:
> Do ye not think th'accomplishment of it
> Sufficient work for one man's simple head,
> All were it, as the rest, but rudely writ?
> How then should I, without another wit,
> Think ever to endure so tedious toil,
> Since that this one is tost with troublous fit
> Of a proud love that doth my spirit spoil.
> Cease then till she vouchsafe to grant me rest,
> Or lend you me another living breast.

The difference between Spenser's treatment of this situation and Sidney's can be expressed, I think, in terms of planes of reality. In Sidney's fifty-third sonnet, 'the people's shouts,' the self-regard of the lover, the war between Cupid and Mars, the imagined power of Stella to make 'a window send forth light' (like Juliet), and her real embarrassment when the lover makes a fool of himself – all these require the viewpoint to dart from plane to plane; the dramatic tensions are created by the comic mismatching of the planes. We know that Spenser is capable of manipulating planes of reality: many of the most telling effects in *The Faerie Queene* are due to a switch from allegorical to human focus – take the contrast between the allegorical nature of Amoret's wound in Book iii canto xii, and her human weakness:

> When her weak feet could scarcely her sustain.

But the effect of the swing from one plane to another here is part of the system of long breathed attention, which links planes without making sharp contrasts between them. In *Amoretti* 33 the alternatives of loving and of finishing *The Faerie Queene* are not dramatically mismatched but matched entirely, as belonging in the same way to the same mind. The situation seems to tremble on the brink of comedy; but the comic potentials are ignored. The ego of the sonnet is identified completely with the author. Lodowick is not used to vary the viewpoint, but is addressed to confirm the unity of the single focus.

We may take another matching pair – Sidney's sonnet 84:

> Highway since you my chief Parnassus be ...

and *Amoretti* 46:

> When my abode's prefixed time is spent,
> My cruel fair straight bids me wend my way;
> But then from heaven most hideous storms are sent,
> As willing me against her will to stay.
> Whom then shall I, or heaven or her obey?
> The heavens know best what is the best for me;
> But as she will, whose will my life doth sway,
> My lower heaven, so it perforce must be.
> But ye high heavens that all this sorrow see,
> Sith all your tempests cannot hold me back,
> Assuage your storms or else both you and she
> Will both together me too sorely wrack.
> Enough it is for one man to sustain
> The storms which she alone on me doth rain.

Both of these are poems in which a journey is moralized in terms of the lady who lies at the beginning or at the end of it. But in

Sidney the playful intensity of the tone – 'I must you of duty greet / With thanks and wishes, wishing thankfully' – is used to create an idea of the lover's mind as happy, keyed-up, self-aware, witty. In Spenser's sonnet the focus is on the external situation; the mind of the lover can be glimpsed only by an analogy with the external world. The ego is the passive and sorrowing victim of the pattern of events. In Sidney's poem the ego imposes on the events: he changes the meaning of the external event, the road, by altering the relationship between it and his mind, by turning it from a despicable subject to the object of his complimentary attention.

The contrast between Spenser's sonnet style and Sidney's is clear and pervasive. Sidney deploys comedy, brusque speech-rhythms, irony, personification, drama, to make his effects. Spenser seeks above all for a blending and smoothing of his materials. The difference is often seen as due simply to temperament. I wish to suggest something more drastic: that the contrast between Spenser and Sidney is one that separates Spenser from all the most successful practitioners of the Petrarchan sonnet in England – Wyatt, Shakespeare, Drayton, as well as Sidney – and shows Spenser running counter to the 'natural genius' of the Elizabethan love sonnet.

I am aware of some temerity in making this point. Josephine Miles[5] has distinguished, throughout English poetry, two modes of syntax, the 'phrasal' or smooth mode (which I take to be Spenser's) and the 'clausal' or predicative one (which I allege to be appropriate to the English sonnet), and has specifically taken the Elizabethan sonnet as a genre which can demonstrate phrasal, clausal, and mixed modes equally well. She quotes the first sonnet of the *Amoretti* ('Happy ye leaves ...') as a good example of the phrasal sonnet, and makes no suggestion that there is any conflict between a phrasal mode and a clausal form. I am unhappy to disagree with so perceptive a reader; but I believe that Miss Miles's description of it as an 'exclamation, not an argument' (page 16) points up the fact that the last two lines imply an argument, which has not in fact taken place:

Leaves, lines, and rhymes, seek her to please alone,
Whom, if ye please, I care for other none.

The simple patterning of *her* (pleased) against *I* (careless about pleasure) suggests the end of a process in which these ideas have been developed in antithesis. But in fact only the lady's capacity for pleasure has been mentioned. The notion of the author's care for his verses appears for the first time in the very last line. I suggest that it is invented at this point (and the situation has many parallels in the *Amoretti*) to give an argumentative form its appropriate conclusion. The tension between the genre and the mode (in Miss Miles's sense) seems to me a recurrent factor in the *Amoretti*. It may even have general significance in the development of the English lyric genius in this period, out of song and into sonnet.

It is well know that Petrarch's rhyme-schemes did not transplant well into English, and that the declamatory and egotistical persona of Wyatt began to modify the Italian form as soon as he touched it. The sonnet form soon began to move towards the three quatrains and a couplet of the standard 'English' type. I believe that the drift towards this new form reflected a pressure which was diffused throughout the English lyric mode at this time – a pressure on the lyric to accommodate drama in miniature, to highlight the persona by oppositions and antitheses, sometimes by dramatic reversals, by concision, by epigrammatic denouements in the final couplet, prepared yet unexpected, giving a final boldness to the whole picture and highlighting the contrary gestures it has contained. Take Shakespeare's sonnet 127:

In the old age black was not counted fair,
Or if it were, it bore not beauty's name;
But now is black beauty's successive heir,
And beauty slandered with a bastard shame.
For since each hand hath put on nature's power,
Fairing the foul with art's false borrowed face,
Sweet beauty hath no name, no holy bower,
But is profaned, if not lives in disgrace.
Therefore my mistress' brows are raven black,
Her eyes so suited, and they mourners seem
At such who, not born fair, no beauty lack,
Slandering creation with a false esteem.
    Yet so they mourn, becoming of their woe,
    That every tongue says beauty should look so.

In such a sonnet a new gesture is made in each quatrain, a new direction is given to thought. In the first stanza we are told of time's degeneration. In the second we hear how the cosmetic powers have usurped nature. In the third we reach the mistress herself who is part of the degenerate modern world (a black beauty) but also part of the opposition to it (mourning for beauty's disgrace). The final couplet solves this riddle and balances the opposites: though she wears the colour of ugliness all are agreed that she looks beautiful. We are aware in reading such a poem of a progressive movement through uncertainty and paradox to a final satisfying expression which picks up and encapsulates the various levels of identification between the poet and the lover. This progressive deployment of tensions and paradoxes towards a final denouement marks the mode of reading for which the English sonnet may be thought to be particularly well adapted. And Spenser's poetic genius stands in direct opposition to it as a mode. The thirty-fourth sonnet of the *Amoretti* is an obvious choice to show how close he can come to the Shakespearian structure:

> Like as a ship that through the ocean wide
> By conduct of some star doth make her way,
> Whenas a storm hath dimmed her trusty guide
> Out of her course doth wander far astray,
> So I, whose star, that wont with her bright ray
> Me to direct, with clouds is overcast,
> Do wander now in darkness and dismay
> Through hidden perils round about me plac'd.
> Yet hope I well that, when this storm is passed,
> My Helice, the loadstar of my life,
> Will shine again and look on me at last
> With lovely light to clear my cloudy grief.
> Till then I wander, careful, comfortless,
> In secret sorrow and sad pensiveness.

Here the direction of each quatrain is reasonably distinct. The first tells of the ship which goes astray when her star is dimmed. The second turns ship into lover and star into mistress. The third moves from despair to hope that the star will shine again. At a superficial level we might seem to be on a Shakespearian course.

But the syntax should give us pause. In Shakespeare it drives forward from one subject-predicate-object proposition to another: Or ... But ... For ... But ... Therefore ... Yet. In Spenser's octave it is characteristically self-involved, with the subject in line 1 only reaching its predicate in line 4 and the new subject in line 5 having to wait for its predicate till line 7. The *Yet* at the beginning of line 9 indicates a real turn or *volta*, but it is the only one in the poem. The final couplet clinches the difference between the poems. Spenser's couplet does not move us into a new plane of sharp relationship between the elements that have appeared. It restates the mood that the situation of the octave has already created. It does not define with sharp finality, but leads us back into the poem, smoothing and further interrelating the connections that already exist.

The form coming to rest on a couplet seems to have posed problems for Spenser that he devised his more successful lyric structures to avoid. In the Spenserian stanza of *The Faerie Queene* the fourth and fifth lines seldom represent a real pause: the fourth line is in an ambiguous relationship to the second; and by their position in the stanza both fourth and fifth tend to be required to make a bridge to some new development in the lines following. The final couplet of the Spenserian stanza is of course turned away from any suggestion of epigrammatic conclusiveness by the disparity of metrical length. The alexandrine seems to turn back, as it were, after it has made its point, and to suggest an arabesque decoration rather than the logical chime of sense. The *Epithalamion* stanza shows the same characteristics. The couplet rhymes are so disposed that they fall normally on lines of unequal length – five feet against three on three occasions, and five against six at the end. The one exception is the *fggf* section, but even there the couplet lines (13 and 14) never mark a pause in the onward flow of sense and rhythm. The same avoidance of couplet cadence is equally a feature of the *Prothalamion*. Not only in his adaptation of the sonnet form but throughout his work Spenser seems to have been anxious to keep the flow of his poetic invention unimpeded by full closes, so that the largest possible area of interconnected meanings can be held in stability, without benefit of the complex subordinating syntax that Milton used for a similar purpose. But even in its Spenserian form the sonnet is rather resistant to such aims. Take the Easter Day sonnet (68) which is, significantly enough, both most akin in mood and method to the *Epithalamion* and also, probably, the best poem in the sequence:

> Most glorious Lord of life, that on this day
> Didst make thy triumph over death and sin,
> And having harrowed hell, didst bring away
> Captivity thence captive, us to win!
> This joyous day, dear Lord, with joy begin;
> And grant that we for whom thou diddest die,
> Being with thy dear blood clean washed from sin,
> May live forever in felicity!
> And that thy love we weighing worthily
> May likewise love thee for the same again,
> And for thy sake, that all like dear didst buy,
> With love may one another entertain!
> So let us love, dear love, like as we ought;[6]
> Love is the lesson which the Lord us taught.

The poem is a tissue of biblical echoes; these and the sacramental occasion (the feast day) are used to enlarge the relationship between the lovers into the analogical relationship between Christ and the world. The sonnet builds the octave very successfully in this way, right up to the climactic line,

> May live forever in felicity!

The parallel and overlapping patterns of life against death, freedom against captivity, joy against purgation, salvation against sin, take their place in a skilful and lucid structure of concepts.

In the sestet, however, the natural turn of the sonnet from its *O altitudo* to a practical conclusion seems to catch Spenser in his own toils. Open invocation gives way to closed relationships; and the spacious movement from God down to man is ensnared when it tries the return from man to God. The loose syntax, characteristic of Spenser, becomes under these circumstances a maze of false starts and dead ends. The multiple puns on 'love' and 'like' differ from those on 'captivity' / 'captive,' 'joy' or 'die' /

'live' in that they seem no longer to have the space to execute their arabesques of pleasure on the surface of a clear meaning; now they have themselves to carry the weight of definition and seem ill at ease with this function. What is the syntax of lines 9 and 10? After much stumbling I have been persuaded that 'grant' in line 6 governs the whole of the third quatrain: 'grant that ... and that thy love we ... And [that we] for thy sake ...' But these relationships are buried in a rhythmical structure which impedes rather than facilitates true reading. The uncertainty of the *thats* in lines 9 and 11 contorts one's sense of the word order. *Likewise* and *the same* in line 10 are also words whose meaning has to be reconstructed from the sense rather than derived from the reading. What does line 11's *all like dear* mean? Sidney Lee modernized *dear* to *deer* – one solution that we need not follow, but a measure of the difficulty. I have come to assume that the best sense is 'all of us at the same price,' but not without stopping and starting. The meaning of the sestet eddies between the several polarities of *thou, we, all, one another, dear love,* but without creating any sense of fluent onward progression.

I comment on these difficulties neither to 'explain' the sonnet (whose general drift is clear enough) nor to convict Spenser of incompetence (for ambiguous syntax need not be a fault). I wish rather to point to a disadvantage apparently imposed on Spenser by the sonnet form – a disadvantage not present when the same material is handled in the stanza form of the *Epithalamion*. In the *Epithalamion* stanzas the dominance of syntax by metrical rhythm is complete. The syntax is loose and aggregative ('phrasal' in Miss Miles's terminology). The sense flows forward, wave after wave of line-length units, till we come to the usual pause at the short lines, and so forward again to the non-epigrammatic and rounding-off final line,

That all the woods may answer and your echo ring.

A sonnet like 68 may manage in the octave to create a spacious effect like that of the *Epithalamion*; but the need to bring the theme to a full point some six lines later denies Spenser the capacity to keep floating his verse forward in the same wave pattern. The need to compress what he is saying leads to a breakdown in the relationship between syntax and verse inside individual lines and to a breakdown in the relationship between line and line, as this is implied by the rhyme-scheme.

Spenser's poetic effects often depend on an unceasing and effortless flow of analogies. At his best this often involves a genuine ambiguity between tenor and vehicle, between the point of comparison and the thing compared. Take the description of Maleger in Book ii canto xi stanza 22 of *The Fairie Queene*:

> As pale and wan as ashes was his look,
> His body lean and meagre as a rake,
> And skin all withered like a dried rook,
> Thereto as cold and dreary as a snake
> That seemed to tremble evermore and quake.
> All in a canvas thin he was bedight
> And girded with a belt of twisted brake;
> Upon his head he wore an helmet light
> Made of a dead man's skull, that seemed a ghastly sight.

Is Maleger a ghost like a man or a man like a ghost? The stanza is not devised to answer such a question. What I take to be its most powerful line ('that seemed to tremble evermore and quake') is powerful in part just because of this ambiguity: we do not know if it is the snakeskin or Maleger's skin that trembles, or indeed if there is a real difference between the two things. An object is built up before our eyes, participating in the nature of many other objects, which has no existence apart from them.

We may take another example (closer to the material of the *Amoretti*) from the description of Belphoebe in Book ii canto iii – say stanza 22, the first stanza of the description:

> Her face so fair as flesh it seemed not,
> But heavenly portrait of bright angel's hue,
> Clear as the sky, withouten blame or blot,
> Through goodly mixture of complexions due;
> And in her cheeks the vermeil red did shew
> Like roses in a bed of lilies shed,
> The which ambrosial odours from them threw
> And gazer's sense with double pleasure fed,
> Able to heal the sick and to revive the dead.

Perhaps the first thing we should notice about this is that it *is* only the first stanza of a description that goes on for another nine – a description which in its ninety lines contains no crystallization into a moral couplet. The material and its valuation grows before our eyes by a confusion of tenor and vehicle that demands the utmost flexibility of reading:

> ... her straight legs ...
> Like two fair marble pillars they were seen,
> Which do the temple of the gods support,
> Whom all the people deck with girlands green,
> And honour in their festival resort.

It is clear that at this point the legs have disappeared and only the pillars remain (the *whom* might indeed suggest that the pillars have also disappeared and that it is the *gods* who are decked). But in the immediately following lines it would be fatal to have the pillars rather than the legs in the front of one's mind:

> Those same with stately grace and princely port
> She taught to tread when she herself would grace,
> But with the woody nymphs when she did play
> Or when the flying libbard she did chase,
> She could them nimbly move and after fly apace.

Belphoebe is not simply a woman like a temple; the reading requires us to be constantly aware that she is both woman and temple, with the values that apply to both these floating freely between their polarities. By such interchange the object grows before us as we read, giving us a sense of generalized discovery rather than of confirmation in sharp focus.

But the English sonnet form, with its epigrammatic structure, seems to fare best when it is analytic of what is accepted rather than synthetic of new vision. The suspensions, the ambiguities of syntax and of analogy that give scope to *The Faerie Queene*, are often merely destructive of order in the *Amoretti*. In sonnet 8, for example, the postponement of the subject of the sentence, *eyes*, and the consequent elaboration of the syntax, seems designed to create a network of analogical relationships, between the lady's eyes (set against the traditional fair lady's eyes) and God's light, and also between angelic flights and Cupid's flights, without defining the nature of the relationships too exactly. But Spenser's evasive methods require more space for this than the sonnet allows; if the English sonnet is going to exploit analogies to their full effect they have to be given a crisper definition. Or take sonnet 17 – the closest to the Belphoebe stanza quoted above:

> The glorious portrait of that angel's face,
> Made to amaze weak men's confused skill,
> And this world's worthless glory to embase,
> What pen, what pencil can express her fill?
> For though he colours could devise at will
> And eke his learned hand at pleasure guide
> Lest trembling it his workmanship should spill,
> Yet many wondrous things there are beside:
> The sweet eye-glances that like arrows glide,
> The charming smiles that rob sense from the heart,
> The lovely pleasance and the lofty pride
> Cannot expressed be by any art.
> A greater craftsman's hand thereto doth need,
> That can express the life of things indeed.

This is one of Spenser's best sonnets; and once again it works by confusing the borderline between physical and spiritual. The elements that the painter 'cannot express' – eye-glances, charming smiles, lofty pride, etc. – are not really unphysical; and it is not in fact true that the artist is wholly incapable of expressing these. The suggestion of 'something beyond' the mere painter is, of course, entirely justified, and the 'many ... things ... beside' at the end of the octave expresses the complementary nature of physical and spiritual with something of the rich evasiveness of the Belphoebe passage. But in the sestet Spenser, as if conscious of the need for simpler categorical distinctions to express real-life relationships, condenses into stricter antithesis ('Cannot expressed be by any art'), setting the physical and the spiritual in a mutually exclusive relationship, which is applied likewise to man and God.

Spenser is unwilling to state unequivocally whether the lady he describes is more real as physical or spiritual entity. But the sonnet is normally expected to end in some clarity of focus. Sidney's sonnets never raise this difficulty. The poem in which he, in his turn, describes the artist's difficulty in expressing the lady –

> What tongue can her perfections tell
> In whose each part all pens may dwell –

is more Ovidian than the *Astrophil and Stella* poems, but the extent to which the fleshly lady is the real lady is not uncharacteristic. It is clear that the ivory, alabaster, cedar, pearl, porphyry, etc. in this poem are ways of expressing the simple human response to flesh. Spenser's ivory, sapphires, rubies, pearl, etc. in *Amoretti* 15 are much more ambiguous in meaning. If, it says, gainful merchants seek for these precious commodities, they need not go to India for them. For these (or their equivalents) can be found in my lady:

> If ivory [you seek] her forehead ivory *ween* [my italics].

Spenser seems to be avoiding the simple statements that her forehead *is* ivory, or that her forehead is *like* ivory; if the merchants' desire of gain points them towards ivory then they might as well be pointed towards her forehead. The ivory is not here a way of talking about white flesh, but an alternative sign for an identical value. The merchants' daughters in the tenth stanza of the *Epithalamion* present another variation on this standard material. The lady, 'virtue's store,' is presented to them as a collection of the usual desirable commodities. The merchants' daughters may stand in amaze, but her 'celestial treasures' are hidden and would amaze them still further. In the spacious structure of the *Epithalamion* there is no need (as I have said above) to bring the analogies to an epigrammatic point. The merchants in sonnet 15 are left with

> that which fairest is, but few behold,
> Her mind adorned with virtues manifold.

The contrast between her mind and the gold, silver, etc. of her body brings the poem to an end without defining the relationship between what is good and what is (evidently) better. In the *Epithalamion* the inside of the lady's mind ('Garnished with heavenly gifts') is catalogued as well as her external worth. Stanza 11 builds up, line by line, the picture of a realm of Grace, corresponding to the realm of Nature in stanza 10. The preference of the merchants' daughters is embedded in a connected and larger system of analogies.

I have hitherto concerned myself mainly with the technical details in which Spenser's mode and the epigrammatic mode of the sonnet are at odds. But it may be proper to face the question why they are so, which Lever poses in his excellent book on the Elizabethan sonnet: 'allegorical romance was one medium, and the sonnet was another. The sonnet, indeed, came into being because a new, personal attitude to experience demanded expression. Why then did Spenser confound the two distinct ways of writing? The answer seems to be that his outlook, grounded upon philosophical idealism, tended to a blurring of the distinction.'[7] Are the *Amoretti* as they are because Spenser's 'philosophical idealism' blurred the individualism of the sonnet tradition against 'allegorical romance'? Neoplatonism is much invoked to explain Spenser's habits of mind and modes of writing; but I am not sure what it means in this context: nothing very precise, I suspect; I can find no reference to points of doctrine in the *Amoretti*. If nothing more is meant than 'a tendency to move rapidly from flesh to spirit' I could not, of course, object; the *Amoretti* is a sequence which often refers to the sanctification of desire. But the interacting of desire and virtue, the carnal and the spiritual, is also a feature of *Astrophil and Stella*. The difference between a sonnet like *Amoretti* 81 ('Fair is my love ...') and *Astrophil and Stella* 71 ('Who will in fairest book of nature ...') is not that one is Neoplatonic and the other not, but that in Spenser the process is one of gradual transformation of the image of the lady from physical to spiritual, whereas in Sidney the two viewpoints are at tension in the mind of the lover. In Spenser the transformation from one angle of vision to another is indeed managed with so much gradualness that it is not at first clear if it has happened at all. It is not immediately clear whether it is her mouth which is praised or her words, nor whether the antithesis in the final

couplet between 'nature's wonderment' and 'heart's astonish-
ment' is one which gives real preference to the latter. But the last
line of the Sidney poem ('But ah, Desire still cries, give me some
food') imparts an unambiguously dramatic power to the an-
tithesis.

Spenser's 'philosophical idealism' does not seem to be, by
itself, a sufficient explanation of the difference between the
Amoretti and *Astrophil and Stella*. One must look further into
Lever's explanation. He implies that Spenser wrote about the
personal situation proper to a sonnet sequence in the style appro-
priate to allegorical romance. But what is the style appropriate to
allegorical romance? In Lever's view it seems to be one which
dissolves the image in favour of the concept: in *The Faerie
Queene*, he says, 'the episodes were enacted on a purely concep-
tual plane. All the allegorical monsters were made of pasteboard,
however brightly painted. There was no reason why the most
ghastly encounters and horrific spectacles should not be re-
counted in a style that remained polished, sonorous and even.'[8] I
take this to be saying that the lady and 'the stresses of real life'[9]
create problems in the *Amoretti* because they cannot dissolve into
their conceptual equivalents with the same ease as the 'pasteboard'
machinery of *The Faerie Queene*. For myself I must feel that the
expression of the problem in terms of the 'reality' of the content
and the 'meaning' of the poems raises too many unknowns. But
if we think of the technique of *The Faerie Queene* not in terms of
allegorical substitution but, with Paul J. Alpers,[10] as a process of
'developing psychological experience within the reader' we may
have terms that allow comparison with the *Amoretti* at a less
daunting level. It seems obvious that the sonnet is not well
adapted to the process that Alpers describes. The sonnet form
demands a quick resolution or sharp point-up of tensions that in
The Faerie Queene remain hanging over the harmony like un-
resolved suspensions in music for stanza after stanza after stanza.
It is not so much, in my view, that Spenser 'blurred' with his
idealism a 'real' situation which would not dissolve; indeed I do
not find the content of the *Amoretti* – that is, the actual situations
created poetically – to be more realistic than that of *The Faerie
Queene*. It is rather that the form demands a sharp relationship

between vision and meaning; the two are not given space to grow into an inter-animating harmony, which is neither figure nor concept, but both.

One may put this in a slightly different way by thinking of the distinction Rosemond Tuve makes in her *Allegorical Imagery* between moralization and allegory.[11] A moralization is a lesson that can be drawn quickly from an image; an allegory has to be lived with and experienced, 'for allegories cannot be arrived at by the shortcut of equations.'[12] The English sonnet form, it seems to me, is suited only to the mode of moralization, the immediate lesson in the final couplet. It cannot aspire to what gives *The Faerie Queene* its power – the allegorical sense of a life lived at the same time on several interlocking but not contrasting planes.

NOTES

1 *Form and Convention in the Poetry of Edmund Spenser*, ed. William Nelson (New York and London, 1961), p. 152.
2 I must admit to being unimpressed by the argument that the *Amoretti* trace a clear and irreversible passage through time, from New Year (4) to New Year (62), Spring (19) to Spring (70) to Winter (89). I am even less willing to believe that this time sequence and that of the *Epithalamion* (see A. Kent Hieatt, *Short Time's Endless Monument*, New York, 1960) form a macrocosmic unity – see Richard Neuse, 'The Triumph over Hasty Accidents: A Note on the Symbolic Mode of the "Epithalamion,"' *MLR* 61 (1966), 163–74.
3 J.W. Lever, *The Elizabethan Love Sonnet* (London, 1956), p. 137.
4 The treatment of *Stella* in the elegies they wrote for *Astrophel*, taken together with the dedication of that volume to Frances Walsingham, gives the evidence for this.
5 Josephine Miles, *Eras and Modes in English Poetry* (London, 1957).
6 It does not seem to have been noticed that *ought* here is probably OED *v*.A.II.2 'Pa.t. of OWE,' or *v*.A.IV.7a, 'perfect tense or passive voice of OWE,' with the sense: 'Let us love one another by the same amount that we have owed [to Christ].'
7 Lever, p. 103.
8 Ibid., pp. 102–3.
9 Ibid., p. 102.
10 Paul J. Alpers, *The Poetry of 'The Faerie Queene'* (Princeton, 1967).
11 Rosemond Tuve, *Allegorical Imagery: Some Medieval Books and Their Posterity* (Princeton, 1966), chap. 1.
12 Ibid., p. 54.

This book

was designed by

ELLEN HUTCHISON

under the direction of

ALLAN FLEMING

University of

Toronto

Press